Best Easy Day Hikes
Seattle

Help Us Keep This Guide Up to Date

Every effort has been made by the author and editors to make this guide as accurate and useful as possible. However, many things can change after a guide is published—trails are rerouted, regulations change, facilities come under new management, etc.

We would love to hear from you concerning your experiences with this guide and how you feel it could be improved and kept up to date. While we may not be able to respond to all comments and suggestions, we'll take them to heart and we'll also make certain to share them with the author. Please send your comments and suggestions to the following address:

> The Globe Pequot Press
> Reader Response/Editorial Department
> P.O. Box 480
> Guilford, CT 06437

Or you may e-mail us at:

> editorial@GlobePequot.com

Thanks for your input, and happy trails!

Best Easy Day Hikes Series

Best Easy Day Hikes
Seattle

Allen Cox

FALCONGUIDES ®

GUILFORD, CONNECTICUT
HELENA, MONTANA
AN IMPRINT OF THE GLOBE PEQUOT PRESS

FALCONGUIDES®

Copyright © 2009 by Morris Book Publishing, LLC

Falcon, FalconGuides, and Outfit Your Mind are registered trademarks
of Morris Book Publishing, LLC.

Layout artist: Kevin Mak
Project manager: John Burbidge

Maps © Morris Book Publishing, LLC

Library of Congress Cataloging-in-Publication Data
Cox, Allen.
 Best easy day hikes Seattle / Allen Cox.
     p. cm. – (Falconguides)
 ISBN 978-0-7627-5118-1
 1. Hiking–Washington (State)–Seattle Region–Guidebooks. 2. Seat-
tle Region (Wash.)–Guidebooks. I. Title.
 GV199.42.W22S423 2009
 796.5109797'77–dc22
                                                2009010711

Printed in the United States of America

10 9 8 7 6 5 4 3 2 1

7.9777

Contents

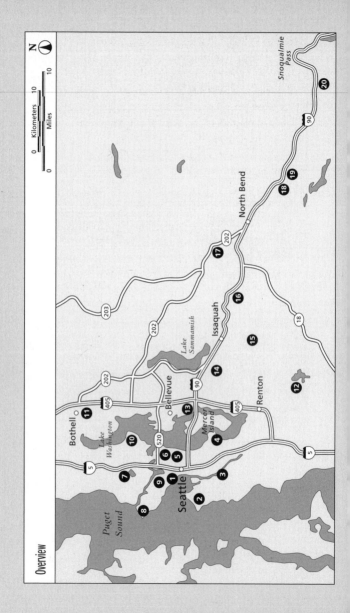

Overview

N

Acknowledgments

First I would like to extend my appreciation to all who advocate for sensible land management and the conservation of public lands and wild habitats. Without their work, few places such as the ones included in this guidebook would be set aside for the rest of us to enjoy.

I would like to thank the land management agencies responsible for the trails included in this guidebook for their cooperation and assistance: Seattle Parks and Recreation, King County Parks, Washington State Parks, Washington State Department of Natural Resources, USDA Forest Service, and University of Washington.

My sincere appreciation goes out to my editor, Scott Adams, and the outstanding team at The Globe Pequot Press for their guidance and clarity in helping me shape this guidebook.

Lastly, I am grateful to Robert Pruett, Roger Ward, and Dana Price, my dear friends and hiking companions, who know how to appreciate an easy day hike better than anyone. Without them, researching this book would have required many lonely hours on the trail.

Introduction

The Lay of the Land—and Water

When you fly into Seattle on a clear day, it appears that there's more water than land. It is a city on and of the water. Puget Sound makes up Seattle's entire western border, and the vast Lake Washington, the eastern. A ship canal slices the city in half as it passes through yet another lake, Lake Union, and connects the two larger bodies of water. The Duwamish River snakes through the city's south end and empties into Elliott Bay—Seattle's busy commercial port.

With Seattle waterlocked on two sides and landlocked on its narrower north and south ends, the only way for the city to grow is up. Neighboring municipalities sprawl north, south, and across Lake Washington, which is spanned by two floating bridges. With all that water, one of Seattle's greatest attributes is its miles of waterfront property, shoreline public space, and dramatic water views.

East across Lake Washington sits another lake nearly as long, Lake Sammamish, with the neighboring cities of Redmond, Bellevue, and Issaquah lining its shores. Beyond that, continuing east and up, the Cascade foothills rise with plenty of land set aside for public use.

What does this landscape do for recreational opportunities in and around the city? If you guessed boating, sailing, swimming, scuba diving, bicycling, jogging, and even parasailing, you'd be correct. But let's not forget about hiking. Seattleites love to hit the trail and take out-of-towners along on the walk. Networks of trails in and around the city offer a variety of settings and terrains, from urban waterfront hikes with stunning views of Seattle's skyline to quiet treks through old-growth forest. The King County Regional Trail System is one of the nation's largest with 175 miles (and growing) of public multiuse trails, so there's a hike in the Seattle area to suit every hiking ability.

This guidebook has attempted to select the best easy day hikes in and around Seattle, all within an hour's drive from downtown and none requiring a ferry ride across Puget Sound.

Seattle-Area Boundaries and Corridors

For the purposes of this guide, the best easy day hikes are located throughout the city and stretch into King County; all are confined to a one-hour drive from downtown Seattle.

Interstate 5 is the main north-south artery through Seattle. From I-5, Interstate 90 and Highway 520 both head east via floating bridges across Lake Washington. The only routes west from Seattle are via ferry service across Puget Sound. None of the hikes in this book are located west of Seattle, and none require ferry transportation from the city. Directions to trailheads are given from either downtown Seattle or one of these three main arteries.

Weather

Seattle enjoys a temperate, generally cool climate with four distinct seasons, few extremes, and an average of fifty-eight days bathed in full sun. The city receives only about 36 inches of annual rainfall over an average 155 days a year. So how did it earn a reputation as one of the wettest U.S. cities when, in fact, it doesn't even rank among the top ten?

Seattle is tucked between the Olympic and Cascade Ranges where clouds gather from the Pacific and can loom for long stretches. When it rains, the city tends to get misted with protracted periods of drizzle. The rainiest seasons are late fall and winter, when torrential Pacific storms occasionally blow through.

There's an old quip about Northwesterners having webbed feet. The truth is that they don't often let a cloudy day or a little drizzle slow them down. Cloudy, wet days in the Pacific Northwest possess their own beauty. The forests glisten and come alive. Fog and mist shroud the hilltops and define contours otherwise not seen. The air is fresh, with grit and dust washed away. With the right gear, you can still enjoy the local trails, whatever the weather.

Part of being prepared for your hike is checking the weather forecast. If weather conditions are potentially hazardous, which is rare, postpone your hike. If weather conditions are favorable to a safe experience on the trail, enjoy yourself, rain or shine.

Wildlife

Wildlife shares the spotlight with Pacific Northwest scenery on trails in and around Seattle. Bald eagles soar over wooded parks and perch in treetops above beaches. Great blue herons strike motionless hunting poses in shoreline shallows. Pileated woodpeckers hammer away at the trunks of decaying trees. Cormorants occupy pilings, their wings spread wide to air-dry after their last dive for a meal.

Birdlife is so abundant in Seattle that bird enthusiast groups conduct annual bird counts in several of Seattle's city parks. Trails in some of these parks are included in this guidebook.

You might spot deer, raccoons, coyotes, and even red foxes near wooded trails. Lucky hikers near Puget Sound have been known to spot seals and sea lions and, on rare occasions, orcas.

Of course it's possible to take a hike in and around Seattle without seeing anything more than a few seagulls. Wildlife doesn't usually stage an entrance just to be noticed by humans. Be on the lookout for the wild inhabitants near the trail and you might be surprised at what critters are watching you.

Encounters with large wildlife are extremely rare but not unheard of, and some trailheads post information about what to do if you encounter a bear or cougar. An excellent source of information regarding such encounters is "Living with Wildlife," available on the Washington Department of Fish and Wildlife Web site at www.wdfw.wa.gov/wlm/living/.

Be Prepared

Hiking in Seattle and the surrounding area is generally safe. Still, you should be prepared, whether you are out for a short urban stroll along Seattle's waterfront or venturing into the more secluded Cascade foothills. The following tips will help you get ready for your hike:

- Research trail conditions in advance by checking the appropriate land management agency's Web site or calling their office.
- Check the weather forecast. If it predicts potentially hazardous weather, postpone your hike.
- Hazards along some trails include uneven footing, steep drop-offs, and slippery trail surfaces, such as mud, ice,

and wet boardwalks. Trekking poles and proper footwear with good tread can help you maintain your balance in more challenging areas.

- Carry a large enough backpack for the essentials and any extras you might want, such as guidebooks, cameras, and binoculars. The essentials are map, compass, water and water filtration method, food, rain gear and extra clothing, matches and fire starter, first-aid kit, army knife or multipurpose tool, flashlight and extra bulbs, and sunscreen and sunglasses. These essentials are especially important on nonurban hikes.

- Know the basics of first aid, including how to treat bleeding, bites, stings, fractures, strains, sprains, and contact with poison oak and stinging nettles. Pack a first-aid kit, no matter how short your excursion.

- While heat stroke and heat exhaustion are unlikely in Seattle's climate, hiking on hot summer days brings risks. Heat exhaustion symptoms include heavy sweating, muscle cramps, headache, dizziness, and fainting. Should you or your companions exhibit any of these symptoms, cool the victim down immediately by rehydrating and getting him or her to an air-conditioned location. Cold showers also help reduce body temperature. Heat stroke is much more serious: The victim may lose consciousness, and the skin is hot and dry to the touch. In this event, call 911 immediately.

- Prepare for extremes of both heat and cold by dressing in layers.

- Regardless of the weather, your body needs water while hiking. A full thirty-two-ounce bottle is the recommended minimum for these short hikes, but more is always better. Bring a full water bottle, whether water is available along the trail or not.

- Don't drink from streams, rivers, creeks, or lakes without first treating or filtering the water. Water from such sources may host a variety of contaminants, including giardia, which can cause serious intestinal unrest.

- Most area trails have cell phone coverage. Bring your device, but make sure you turn it off or put it on the vibrate setting if you are hiking in a place where a cell phone ring might disturb wildlife or fellow hikers.

- Make sure children don't stray from the designated route. Children should carry a whistle; if they become lost, they should stay in one place and blow the whistle to summon help.

- Many of the waterfront hikes in this book are not safe for swimming. Swim at designated swimming beaches only, with a companion and preferably a lifeguard present.

Zero Impact

Trails in the Seattle area are heavily used year-round. We, as trail users and advocates, must be especially vigilant to make sure our passage leaves no lasting mark. Here are some basic guidelines for preserving trails:

- Pack out all your own trash, including biodegradable items like orange peels, or deposit it in a designated trash container. You might also pack out garbage left by less considerate hikers.

- Don't approach or feed wildlife—the squirrel eyeing your energy bar is best able to survive if it remains self-reliant.

- Don't pick wildflowers or gather rocks or other treasures along the trail. Removing these items will only take away from the next hiker's experience.

- Stay on the established route to avoid damaging trailside soils and plants. This is also a good rule of thumb for avoiding poison oak and stinging nettle, common regional trailside irritants.

- Don't create shortcuts, which can promote erosion and damage native vegetation.

- Be courteous by not making loud noises while hiking.

- Many of these trails are multiuse, which means you'll share them with other hikers, runners, skaters, bicyclists, and equestrians. Familiarize yourself with the proper trail etiquette. As a pedestrian, you generally have the right-of-way, but you should yield when common sense dictates.

- Use restrooms and outhouses at trailheads or along the trail.

Land Management

The following organizations manage most of the public lands described in this guide and can provide further information on these and other trails in their service areas:

- Seattle Parks and Recreation, 100 Dexter Avenue North, Seattle 98109; (206) 684-4075, TTY (206) 233-1509; www.seattle.gov/parks/. A complete listing of city parks, information about park facilities, and maps for most parks are available on the Web site.

- Port of Seattle, P.O. Box 1209, Seattle 98111; (206) 728-3000; www.portseattle.org.

- King County Parks, 201 South Jackson Street, Suite 700, Seattle 98104; (206) 296-8687; www.kingcounty .gov/recreation/parks.aspx. A complete listing of county parks and information about park facilities and trails are available on the Web site.

- Washington Park Arboretum, University of Washington, P.O. Box 358010, Seattle 98195-8010; (206) 543-8800; www.depts.washington.edu/wpa.

- Washington State Parks, 1111 Israel Road SW, Tumwater 98504-2650; (360) 902-8844; www.parks.wa.gov.

- State of Washington Department of Natural Resources, P.O. Box 47000, Olympia 98504-7000; (360) 902-1000; www.dnr.wa.gov.

- USDA Forest Service, Mt. Baker–Snoqualmie National Forest, 222 Yale Avenue North, 98109-5429; Outdoor Recreation Information: (206) 470-4060; www.fs.fed .us/r6/mbs. Trail information and maps are available on the Web site.

Public Transportation

This guidebook includes driving directions to trailheads but does not include information on public transportation routes, schedules, or fares. King County Metro Transit provides transit service to or near most trailheads in this book. For information call Metro Transit at (800) 542-7876 or (206) 553-3000, or visit http://transit.metrokc.gov.

How to Use This Guide

This guide is designed to be simple and easy to use. Each hike is described with a map and summary information that delivers the trail's vital statistics, including length, difficulty, fees and permits, park hours, canine compatibility, and trail contacts. Directions to the trailhead are also provided with trailhead GPS coordinates, along with a general description of what you'll see along the way. A detailed route finder (Miles and Directions) provides mileages between significant landmarks along the trail.

Hike Selection

This guide describes trails that are accessible to every hiker. The longest hike is less than 6 miles round-trip, and most are considerably shorter. They range in difficulty level from flat excursions perfect for a family outing to more challenging hikes in the Cascades with some elevation gain. These trails were selected to represent a wide diversity of terrain, scenery, and experiences. Keep in mind that nearby trails, often in the same park or preserve, may offer options better suited to your needs and abilities. These hikes are spaced throughout the Seattle area—wherever your starting point, you'll find a great easy day hike nearby.

Difficulty Ratings

These are all easy hikes, but easy is a relative term. In the Seattle area, hills are a fact of life, but many of the hikes in this guide have no elevation gain at all; others have moderate elevation gain.

To aid in the selection of a hike that suits your particular needs and abilities, each hike is rated easy, moderate, or more challenging. Bear in mind that even most challenging routes can be made easier by hiking within your limits, being prepared, using trekking poles, and resting when you need to.

- **Easy** hikes are generally short and flat, taking no longer than an hour or two to complete.
- **Moderate** hikes involve increased distance and/or slight changes in elevation or may take longer than one to two hours to complete.
- **More challenging** hikes feature some steep stretches, more elevation gain, greater distances, or may take longer than two hours to complete.

These ratings are subjective. What you consider easy is entirely dependent on your level of fitness and the adequacy of your gear (primarily shoes). If you are hiking with a group, you should select a hike with a rating that's appropriate for the least fit and least prepared hiker in your party.

Approximate hiking times are based on the assumption that on flat ground, most walkers average 2.5 miles per hour. Adjust that rate by the steepness of the terrain and your level of fitness (subtract time if you're an aerobic animal; add time if you're hiking with kids or are easily distracted by trailside attractions), and you will arrive at an approximate hiking duration. Be sure to add more time if you plan to take part in other activities, such as picnicking, bird-watching, or photography.

Trail Finder

Map Legend

═══〈5〉═══	Interstate Highway
══〈18〉══	State Highway
═══════	Local Roads
= = = = = =	4WD Roads
▬▬▬▬▬▬	Featured Trail
- - - - - -	Trail
┼─┼─┼─┼─┼	Railroad
～～～～	River/Creek
⁓ ⁓ ⁓	Marsh/Swamp
⬭	Ocean/Lake
▭ ▭	Local Park/Golf Course
▬ ▬	State Park
⬈	Boat Launch
•—•	Gate
‿	Bridge
🕯	Lighthouse
▯	Observation Tower
🅿	Parking
▲	Peak
■	Point of Interest/Structure
▥	Restroom
○	Town
⓫	Trailhead
◪	Viewpoint/Overlook
⋙	Waterfall
N ⬇	True North (Magnetic North is approximately 15.5° East)

1 Myrtle Edwards Park to Elliott Bay Park

This urban bayside hike near Seattle's busy waterfront follows a flat, paved path past landscaped gardens and world-class sculptures. The trail traverses two adjoining shoreline parks, the entire length showcasing spectacular city, bay, mountain, and island views, with plenty of opportunities to spot marine wildlife.

Distance: 3.4 miles out and back

Approximate hiking time: 1.5 hours

Difficulty: Easy, flat trail

Trail surface: Paved

Best season: Year-round

Other trail users: Foot traffic only; runs parallel to a designated bike path

Canine compatibility: Leashed dogs permitted

Fees and permits: No fees or permits required

Schedule: Open daily. Myrtle Edwards Park is open twenty-four hours a day; Elliott Bay Park is open 6:00 a.m. to 11:00 p.m.

Maps: USGS Seattle South R and Seattle North R; Seattle street map

Trail contacts: Myrtle Edwards Park, Seattle Parks and Recreation, (206) 684-4075; www.seattle.gov/parks

Elliott Bay Park, Port of Seattle, (206) 728-3000; www.portseattle.org/community/resources/parks/index.shtml

Finding the trailhead: The trail is accessible from the north or south end. The south trailhead is located on the waterfront at the foot of Broad Street and is the best access point for those who are downtown on foot. Hikers wanting free parking should begin the hike at the north trailhead at the opposite end of the park. To access the

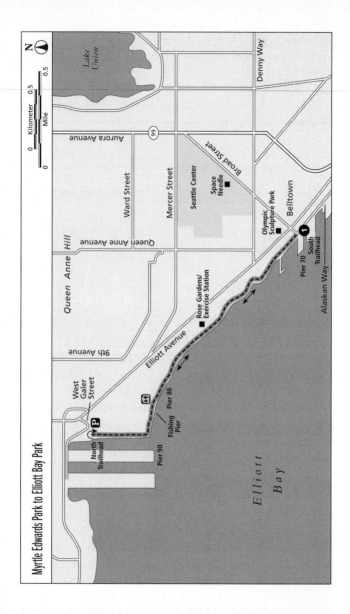

Myrtle Edwards Park to Elliott Bay Park

north trailhead from downtown, drive north on Elliott Avenue. Turn left onto West Galer Street, and turn left after 1 short block. The street ends at the park's parking lot. GPS: N47 36.91' / W122 21.31' (south trailhead); N47 37.95' / W122 22.70' (north trailhead)

The Hike

The Myrtle Edwards Park to Elliott Bay Park Trail was designed to showcase the best of Seattle's scenery—downtown skyscrapers, the iconic Space Needle, Puget Sound, Seattle's busy port, Bainbridge Island, the Olympic Mountains, and Mt. Rainier—and it does not disappoint.

The south trailhead begins at the fountain between Pier 70 and Seattle Art Museum's Olympic Sculpture Park. If you have an extra half hour to spare, touring this free-admission outdoor sculpture park is a great way to either begin or end your hike.

The shoreline trail through these narrow parks is paved and flat and parallels a bicycle path among acres of grassy hillocks, landscaped gardens, picnic tables, benches, and sculptures.

Approximately midpoint up the trail, you pass a sign that welcomes you to Elliott Bay Park, but not to worry—you're not lost. Elliott Bay Park, managed by the Port of Seattle, is a seamless extension of Myrtle Edwards Park, which is managed by Seattle Parks and Recreation and named in honor of Myrtle Edwards, a former member of the Seattle City Council who championed the conservation of much of the city's land as public space.

Continuing north, you come to a formal rose garden surrounded by a boxwood hedge. Beside the garden, an outdoor exercise station is waiting for those compelled to add some push-ups, pull-ups, or crunches to their hike.

Beyond the rose garden, you pass the Port of Seattle's Pier 86 Grain Terminal and then the Elliott Bay Fishing Pier, where you can watch people pull in the catch of the day. You'll find restrooms, a water fountain, and vending machines here.

The trail continues north along Pier 90's waterway to a parking lot and the alternative (north) trailhead for this hike. Turn around and retrace your steps back to the starting point.

Miles and Directions

0.0 Start at the south trailhead, which begins at Pier 70.

1.0 Come to a sign for Elliott Bay Park.

1.2 Pass the Elliott Bay Fishing Pier.

1.7 Reach the parking lot and Pier 90 trailhead. Retrace your steps.

3.4 Arrive back at Pier 70.

2 Alki Trail

Alki Beach is the birthplace of Seattle, where a schooner set the first settlers ashore in November 1851. Today this long stretch of shoreline and beach is one of Seattle's liveliest and most scenic neighborhoods, where people come to play, dine, stroll, and scuba dive. If you've ever seen a postcard of Seattle's stunning skyline shot from across the harbor, the classic photo was likely taken from the starting point of this hike.

Distance: 4.6 miles out and back

Approximate hiking time: 2 to 2.5 hours

Difficulty: Moderate due to distance

Trail surface: Paved

Best season: Year-round

Other trail users: Bicycles and skaters on a parallel trail

Canine compatibility: Leashed dogs permitted

Fees and permits: No fees or permits required

Schedule: Open twenty-four hours daily

Maps: USGS Seattle South W and Seattle South E; Seattle street map

Trail contacts: Seattle Parks and Recreation, (206) 684-4075; www.seattle.gov/parks

Finding the trailhead: From northbound or southbound Interstate 5, take exit 163 (West Seattle Bridge). Take the Harbor Avenue SW exit off the bridge and drive north on Harbor Avenue SW to Seacrest Park at 1660 Harbor Avenue SW. Free parking is available in the lot or on the street. Summer season parking can be difficult. GPS: N47 35.35' / W122 22.89'

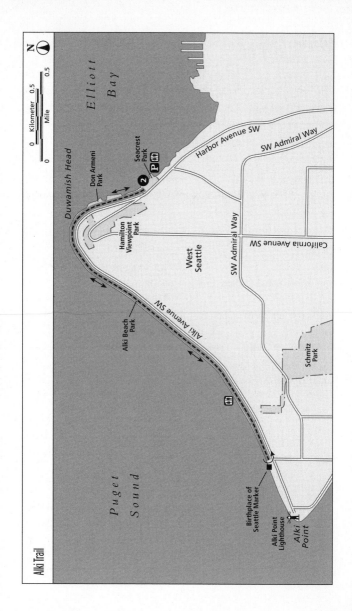

Alki Trail

Puget Sound

Elliott Bay

Duwamish Head

Don Armeni Park

Seacrest Park

2

P

Hamilton Viewpoint Park

West Seattle

Harbor Avenue SW

SW Admiral Way

SW Admiral Way

California Avenue SW

Alki Beach Park

Alki Avenue SW

Schmitz Park

Birthplace of Seattle Marker

Alki Point Lighthouse

Alki Point

0   Kilometer   0.5

0   Mile   0.5

N

The Hike

The Alki Trail follows West Seattle's Harbor Avenue SW and Alki Avenue SW along Puget Sound in one of the city's most scenic areas. The trail passes through several parks, the largest of which is Alki Beach Park.

This hike takes in the most scenic segment of the trail, beginning at Seacrest Park, a spot popular with scuba divers, where you will find a pier, boathouse, restaurant, and restrooms. The focal point is the full frontal view of the Seattle skyline across Elliott Bay.

Walking north, you soon pass Don Armeni Park and Boat Ramp and, beyond that, Duwamish Head, where the trail veers to the left to round the head. The pier at Duwamish Head is a great place to pause and take in the view, which opens up at this point to include Puget Sound as it stretches north and Bainbridge Island and the Olympic Mountains (on a clear day) to the west.

After rounding Duwamish Head, the trail continues southwest along the seawall on Alki Avenue SW. On the opposite side of the street, tiny beach cottages are nestled between modern luxury condos. At the beginning of the commercial district, with its many restaurants, the seawall ends and the beach widens, allowing you a choice of hiking on pavement or sand. You will pass a community center building, a picnic shelter with several tables, and a miniature replica of the Statue of Liberty.

A short distance beyond, near the end of the public beach, a historical marker commemorates the spot where the Denny Party (Seattle's founders) first came ashore on a stormy November day in 1851. This is the hike's turn-around point.

Option: To add more miles of Puget Sound scenery to your hike, continue along Alki Avenue SW a few more blocks for views of the working lighthouse at Alki Point and even farther around the point for expansive views to the south across the Sound to Vashon Island.

Miles and Directions

0.0 Start at Seacrest Park and walk north toward Duwamish Head and Alki Beach.

0.3 Pass Don Armeni Park and Boat Ramp.

0.5 The trail veers left to round Duwamish Head.

1.0 Reach the commercial district.

2.3 Reach the BIRTHPLACE OF SEATTLE marker, your turnaround point.

4.6 Arrive back at Seacrest Park.

3 Camp Long

Camp Long is a woodland retreat inside Seattle's city limits. This sixty-eight-acre park borders the West Seattle Golf Course and boasts miles of hiking trails, the first artificial climbing rock in North America, an environmental education center located in an old lodge, several rustic vacation rental cabins, and enough wildlife to attract hundreds of birders for an annual bird count.

Distance: 1.3-mile loop
Approximate hiking time: 1 hour
Difficulty: Moderate due to a 15 percent grade on sections of the trail and a 400-foot elevation gain
Trail surface: Soil, gravel
Best season: Year-round
Other trail users: None
Canine compatibility: Leashed dogs permitted
Fees and permits: No fees or permits required

Schedule: Open 10:00 a.m. to 6:00 p.m.; March through October, open Tuesday through Sunday; November through February, open Tuesday through Saturday
Maps: USGS Seattle South W and Seattle South E; Camp Long trail map, available at the park office; Seattle street map
Trail contacts: Seattle Parks and Recreation, (206) 684-4075; www.seattle.gov/parks

Finding the trailhead: From Interstate 5, take exit 163 (West Seattle Bridge). Stay on the bridge, which becomes Fauntleroy Way SW. Follow Fauntleroy as it curves to the left up the hill, and turn left onto 35th Avenue SW (the first light). Turn left onto SW Dawson Street to enter the park. GPS: N47 33.35' / W122 22.51'

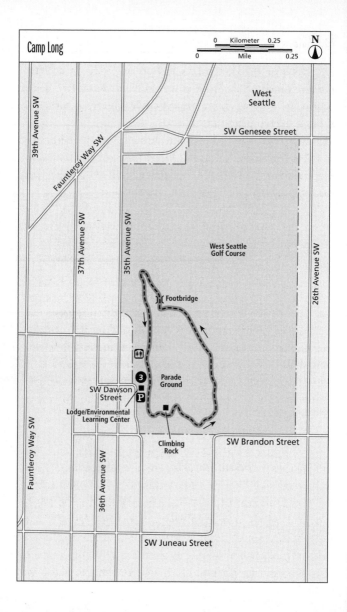

Camp Long

0   Kilometer   0.25

0   Mile   0.25

N

West Seattle

SW Genesee Street

39th Avenue SW

Fauntleroy Way SW

37th Avenue SW

35th Avenue SW

West Seattle Golf Course

26th Avenue SW

Footbridge

Parade Ground

3

SW Dawson Street

Lodge/Environmental Learning Center

Climbing Rock

SW Brandon Street

Fauntleroy Way SW

36th Avenue SW

SW Juneau Street

The Hike

The creation of Camp Long began in 1937 as a WPA project designed for public use as well as a Boy Scout retreat. Its mission was to bring people close to nature, one it has achieved many times over.

Before you begin your hike through Camp Long, stop at the information desk in the lodge and pick up a free park map. Although most of the trails are well marked, a park map will help you navigate the few that aren't.

The trailhead begins at the right of the lodge. Head down the stairs to the Parade Ground and turn right. At the far end of the lawn you pass a fire pit and, beyond that, come to Schurman Rock, the first artificial climbing rock in North America, which was dedicated along with Camp Long in 1941. If you're a rock-climbing enthusiast, this is a rare opportunity to test your skill on a near antique.

Turn right at Schurman Rock and follow the Longfellow Creek Trail into the forest and down the ravine. In just over 0.25 a mile, come to a signed fork in the trail. Follow the Lower Loop Trail (straight ahead), which eventually begins to ascend. Several species of birds live in this forest; be on the lookout for which ones you can spot.

At about 0.75 mile into the hike, come to a wooden footbridge across Longfellow Creek on your right and cross the bridge. In a short distance, come to a convergence of trails with stairs straight ahead, another footbridge to the left, and an unmarked, well-maintained trail (Animal Tracks Nature Trail) on your right that continues up the hill. Turn right onto Animal Tracks Nature Trail. At the top of the hill, the trail hairpins sharply to the left and reaches a bench. This is a peaceful place to catch your breath and enjoy the silence of the forest. You might even be lucky enough to spot one of the resident owls or an eagle.

Continuing on, you come out of the forest and pass Polliwog Pond on the edge of the Parade Ground. At the center point of the Parade Ground, turn right and follow the stairs back up to the lodge and the trailhead.

Miles and Directions

0.0 Start at the trailhead immediately to the right of the lodge. Head down the stairs to the Parade Ground and turn right. Follow the trail around the lawn past the fire pit to Schurman Rock.

0.2 Turn right at Schurman Rock and follow the trail signs to Longfellow Creek Trail.

0.5 Follow the sign to Lower Loop Trail.

0.7 Turn right and cross the footbridge.

0.8 Turn right and follow Animal Tracks Nature Trail (unmarked).

1.3 Arrive back at the lodge.

4 Seward Park Loop

Seward Park juts into Lake Washington like a thumb. Seattle city officials had the foresight to acquire the wild, wooded property in 1892 and eventually turn it into the public space we enjoy today. The loop trail circles the park on a closed-off service road for most of its length, with the lake on one side and Seattle's largest remaining old-growth forest on the other.

Distance: 2.4-mile loop
Approximate hiking time: 1 hour
Difficulty: Easy, flat trail
Trail surface: Paved
Best season: Year-round
Other trail users: Bicyclists, skaters
Canine compatibility: Leashed dogs permitted

Fees and permits: No fees or permits required
Schedule: Open daily, 6:00 a.m. to 10:00 p.m.
Maps: USGS Seattle South E and Bellevue South W; Seattle street map
Trail contacts: Seattle Parks and Recreation, (206) 684-4075; www.seattle.gov/parks

Finding the trailhead: From Interstate 5 take exit 163 (South Columbian Way). Follow South Columbian Way to Beacon Avenue South and turn right. Take the first left onto Orcas Avenue South and follow it until it becomes Lake Washington Boulevard South and, curving right, ends in Seward Park. The trailhead is beside the Art Studio building. GPS: N47 33.11' / W122 15.42'

The Hike

Lake Washington—a 20-mile-long lake lined with waterfront homes and parks—defines Seattle's eastern boundary. One of the city's most beautiful parks, Seward Park occupies Bailey

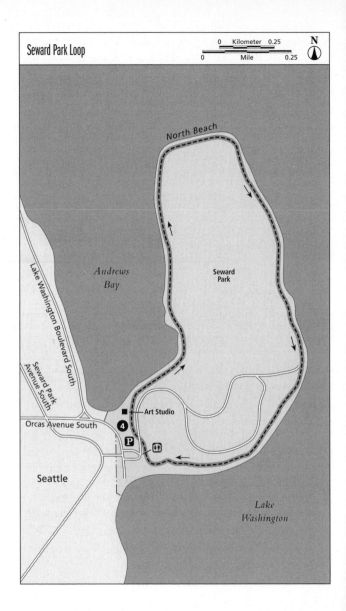

Seward Park Loop

0   Kilometer   0.25

0   Mile   0.25

N

North Beach

Andrews
Bay

Seward
Park

Lake Washington Boulevard South

Seward Park Avenue South

Orcas Avenue South

Art Studio

P

Seattle

Lake
Washington

Peninsula and is home to an environmental and Audubon center, a clay art studio, an amphitheater, picnic facilities, and miles of trails. The longest and most scenic of the park's trails is the Seward Park Loop (trail #10 on the park's official map, available on their Web site). This wide, paved trail doubles as a service road that is closed to motorized public traffic.

The trailhead for this hike is at the edge of the lake near the art studio. As you skirt the perimeter of the peninsula, it's easy to forget that you're still connected to the mainland. The setting has the distinctive feel of an island. In fact, Seward Park once was an island; it became attached to the mainland when the building of the locks on the ship canal lowered Lake Washington's water level.

The trail leads to a fishing pier and a wide swimming beach and lawn before rounding North Beach at the tip of the peninsula. Here Mercer Island, with its luxury waterfront homes and forested hillside neighborhoods, comes into full view.

The trail narrows from a service road to a wide footpath in its ending stretch. If it's a clear day—or at least one with a high enough cloud cover—you will be rewarded with an unobstructed view of massive Mt. Rainier dominating the horizon about 70 miles to the south.

Miles and Directions

0.0 Start at the trailhead next to the Seward Park Art Studio for a clockwise loop. **Option:** To follow the loop in a counterclockwise direction, start at the parking lot at the end of Lake Washington Boulevard South.

0.7 Pass a fishing pier and swimming beach.

1.7 The trail narrows to a footpath.

2.4 Arrive back at the art studio trailhead.

5 Volunteer Park

Volunteer Park crowns Seattle's Capitol Hill, offering winding paths through lawns with formal gardens and a diverse collection of mature trees—a prime example of elegant, early landscape design and perfect for a slow stroll or a half-hour hike. This popular city park is home to the Seattle Asian Art Museum, the Volunteer Park Conservatory, and a brick water tower that offers an unsurpassed 360-degree view of Seattle from atop its 106 steps.

Distance: 1.0-mile loop
Approximate hiking time: 30 minutes without visiting the attractions
Difficulty: Easy, flat, and gently sloped trail
Trail surface: Paved, dirt
Best season: Year-round
Other trail users: Bicyclists, skaters

Canine compatibility: Leashed dogs permitted
Fees and permits: No fees or permits required
Schedule: Open year-round, 6:00 a.m. to 11:00 p.m.
Maps: USGS Seattle North E; Seattle street map
Trail contacts: Seattle Parks and Recreation, (206) 684-4075; www.seattle.gov/parks

Finding the trailhead: From downtown Seattle drive east on Olive Way over the Interstate 5 overpass. Follow East Olive Way as it curves left up the hill and become East John Street. Follow East John Street to Broadway East and turn left. Broadway East becomes 10th Avenue East. Turn right at East Prospect, following the signs to the Asian Art Museum. Turn left at 14th Avenue East to enter Volunteer Park. You can begin your hike anywhere, but the suggested starting point is in front of the Seattle Asian Art Museum. GPS: N47 37.81' / W122 18.90'

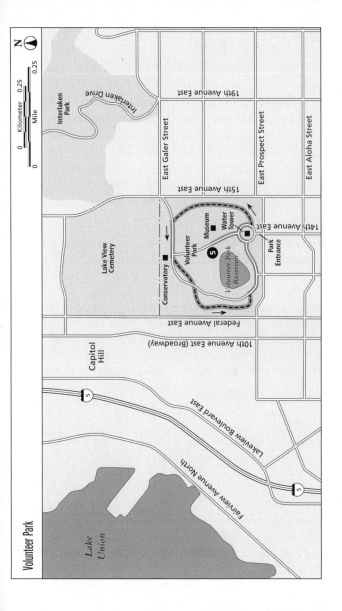

Volunteer Park

The Hike

At the turn of the twentieth century, the City of Seattle hired the Olmsted Brothers, internationally renowned landscape architects, to design many of the city's parks. Volunteer Park was their crowning achievement in the city, integrating formal design elements with the natural environment.

Since this park is relatively small, you can easily explore it without a trail map or directions. The route prescribed here circles the entire park in a short hike that allows you to take in the key attractions.

Begin your hike in front of the Asian Art Museum. Across the drive and parking lot, overlooking the city, you'll notice one of Seattle's classic postcard views: a black doughnut-shaped sculpture (Isamu Noguchi's Black Sun) with the Space Needle, Puget Sound, and the Olympic Mountains in the distance.

Facing the museum, walk to the right, toward the water tower. Circle the tower (don't exit the park) and find the unpaved path on the left. Across the street sit some of Seattle's stateliest historic homes.

Turn left onto the path, which arcs down the hill and veers to the left (northward) through expansive sloping lawns and mature shade trees before heading back up the slope to the Volunteer Park Conservatory. Built in 1912, the conservatory houses a vast collection of temperate, arid, and tropical plant specimens and is worth a visit. (The conservatory is open daily from 10:00 a.m. to 4:00 p.m.; open until 6:00 p.m. in summer.)

Facing the conservatory, follow the unpaved path down the hill beside the drive. Cross the drive and descend the stairs to the left and follow the lawn below the drive. At the street, climb the stairs on the left. Join the paved path beside the drive, and follow the drive uphill toward the water tower. The reservoir, constructed in 1901, is on your left.

The medieval-looking brick water tower stands on the summit of one of Seattle's highest hills. For a free panorama that rivals the $16 trip up the Space Needle, climb the water tower's 106 steps and savor the view of city, water, islands, and mountains.

Immediately to the north of the water tower, you arrive back at the Seattle Asian Art Museum, a beautiful example of art deco architecture. Since this was a short hike, reward yourself with a tour of the museum. For more information call (206) 654-3100 or visit www.seattleartmuseum.org/ visit/visitSAAM.asp.

Miles and Directions

0.0 Start in front of the Asian Art Museum. Facing the museum, walk to the right (south) past the water tower and turn left onto the dirt path.

0.4 Reach the Volunteer Park Conservatory. Facing the conservatory, follow the unpaved path down the hill.

1.0 Arrive back at your starting point in front of the museum.

6 Arboretum Waterfront Trail

A ship canal slices Seattle in half, connecting Puget Sound to Lake Washington. At the lake end of the canal, the Arboretum Waterfront Trail follows the marshy shoreline across two islands with views across Union Bay to the University of Washington and Husky Stadium. It is part of a larger network of trails through the 230-acre Washington Park Arboretum and offers an up-close glimpse of marshland flora and fauna, making this easy trail a hit with wildlife photographers.

Distance: 0.9 mile out and back
Approximate hiking time: 30 minutes
Difficulty: Easy, flat trail
Trail surface: Soil, bark, concrete and metal grate footbridges
Best season: Year round
Other trail users: None
Canine compatibility: Leashed dogs permitted

Fees and permits: No fees or permits required
Schedule: Open daily from dawn to dusk
Maps: USGS Seattle North E; Seattle street map
Trail contacts: Washington Park Arboretum, University of Washington, (206) 543-8800; www.depts.washington.edu/wpa

Finding the trailhead: From Interstate 5 take exit 168 and merge onto Highway 520 East. Take the first exit (Montlake Boulevard). Immediately across Montlake Boulevard, make a slight right at Lake Washington Boulevard East and turn left at 24th Avenue East. Follow the signs to McCurdy Park and the Museum of History and Industry (MOHAI). Park in the lower lot behind the museum and look for a trailhead kiosk near the lakeshore. GPS: N47 38.75' / W122 17.98'

Arboretum Waterfront Trail

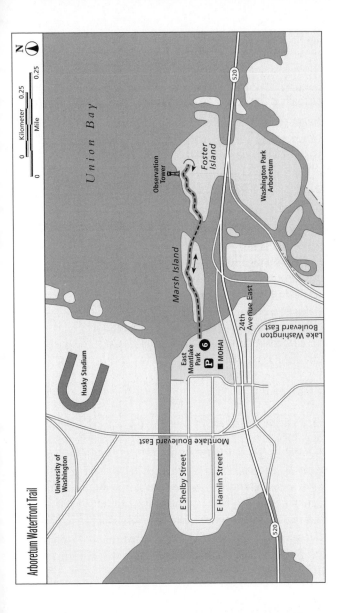

The Hike

For many Seattleites, the Arboretum Waterfront Trail is a favorite. Its short length offers a quick, accessible break from city life. Footbridges carry a sizable length of the route over the water, giving the trail a unique character. Views of the university, passing boat traffic, and the abundant waterfowl that make the marshes their home give hikers plenty to look at; binoculars or a camera come in handy on this hike.

Begin the trail at the kiosk at the water's edge behind the Museum of History and Industry. The kiosk displays an excellent map of the trail. Follow the trail to the right. Almost immediately, the trail crosses a footbridge to Marsh Island, where the raised bark–covered trail keeps your boots dry as it cuts through low, marshland woods and along the lakeshore. A few short spur trails lead to tucked-away concrete floats that are great spots for hikers to stop and view the lake activity as well as docking spots for kayakers and canoers.

As you hike this trail, you may be aware of the rush of traffic on nearby Route 520 as it flows onto the Evergreen Point Floating Bridge. The traffic doesn't seem to deter hikers, as evidenced by the trail's heavy use.

The trail leads across a bridge from Marsh Island to Foster Island. On Foster much of the trail is built on a network of bridges that lead you away from shore for a duck's–eye view of the marshy shoreline. This is one of the most interesting features of the trail and is a great place to spot a variety of waterfowl. After the bridge, a short spur trail leads to a raised viewing platform that offers superb views of the ship canal, Lake Washington, the University of Washington, and the waterfront homes of the Laurelhurst district across Union Bay.

Continuing on the main trail for a short distance brings you to the end of the Arboretum Waterfront Trail and the beginning of the trail that leads farther into the arboretum. Turn around at this point and retrace your steps back to the trailhead, or continue on for a further exploration of the 230-acre park.

Miles and Directions

0.0 Start at the kiosk near the lakeshore. Facing the kiosk, the trail leads to the left or the right. Follow the trail to the right.

0.5 Reach a kiosk where the trail leaves the marsh and enters an open grassy area. Turn around here and retrace your steps. **Option:** For an extended hike, continue following this trail to the right to reach a larger network of Washington Park Arboretum trails.

0.9 Arrive back at the starting point kiosk.

7 Green Lake

Green Lake Park is nestled in North Seattle's urban Green Lake neighborhood. The centerpiece of this 300-plus–acre park is the lake itself, which is surrounded by a 2.8-mile path. This popular park, one of the city's outdoor recreation hotspots, sits adjacent to Woodland Park, home of the Woodland Park Zoo.

Distance: 2.8-mile loop
Approximate hiking time: 1.5 hours
Difficulty: Easy, flat trail
Trail surface: Paved and gravel
Best season: Year round
Other trail users: Bicyclists, skaters, runners
Canine compatibility: Leashed dogs permitted

Fees and permits: No fees or permits required
Schedule: Open daily, twenty-four hours a day
Maps: USGS Seattle North E; Seattle street map
Trail contacts: Seattle Parks and Recreation, (206) 684-4075; www.seattle.gov/parks

---

Finding the trailhead: Because the Green Lake Trail is a loop, you can begin at any point. The following directions are for parking and beginning the hike at the south end of the lake. From downtown take Interstate 5 north to exit 169 (Northeast 50th Street) and turn left onto Northeast 50th. Turn right onto Green Lake Way North and then veer left onto West Green Lake Way North. Just past the Par 3 Golf Course, park in the first lot on either side of the street. GPS: N47 40.32' / W122 20.62'

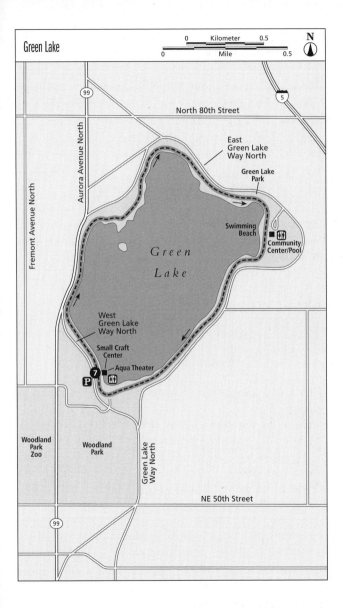

Green Lake

| 0 | Kilometer | 0.5 |
| 0 | Mile | 0.5 |

N

North 80th Street

Aurora Avenue North

Fremont Avenue North

East
Green Lake
Way North

Green Lake
Park

Green Lake

Swimming
Beach

Community
Center/Pool

West
Green Lake
Way North

Small Craft
Center

Aqua Theater

7

P

Woodland
Park
Zoo

Woodland
Park

Green Lake
Way North

NE 50th Street

99

The Hike

The same glacial ice sheet that scooped out Puget Sound also created Green Lake approximately 50,000 years ago. Today Green Lake occupies the bulk of a graceful city park containing an array of athletic and recreational facilities and a loop trail. You can begin the hike at any point on the trail, but for a frame of reference, assume the trail begins at the Green Lake Small Craft Center at the south end of the lake and that you will hike in a clockwise direction.

This easy 2.8-mile trail is one of the city's most popular spots for walking, jogging, and people watching. The trail hugs the shore among rolling lawns, cattails, and a variety of mature shade trees, with pleasant views across the water to the park's greenery and the hillside neighborhoods beyond.

In just short of a mile, you come to the Seattle Public Theater at the Bathhouse, an active stage theater housed in a converted 1928 bathhouse. A swimming beach is located behind the building.

At about the 1.8-mile mark, pass the Green Lake Park Community Center, complete with pool, indoor basketball court, athletic fields, tennis courts, boat rentals, concessions, swimming beach, restrooms, and fishing dock.

Near the end of the loop and the Par 3 Golf Course, you pass a piece of true Seattle kitsch: Green Lake Aqua Theater, the relic of a once 5,500-seat lakeside amphitheater. Circa 1950 the amphitheater was home to an aquatic theater troupe that performed lavishly staged "swimusicals"—musical theater complete with water ballet, high dives, and show tunes emanating from a floating orchestra pit (think Esther Williams films). Today the portion of Aqua Theater that remains is part of the adjacent Small Craft Center.

Round the bend a short distance, and you are back at the starting point.

Miles and Directions

0.0 Start at the south end of the lake at the Small Craft Center. Facing the lake, turn left to go clockwise around the loop.

0.9 Pass the bathhouse theater.

1.8 Pass the Green Lake Park Community Center.

2.7 Pass the aqua theater remnants.

2.8 Arrive back at your starting point.

8 Discovery Park Loop

Occupying 534 acres atop Seattle's Magnolia Bluff, Discovery Park is Seattle's largest. The first European ship to explore Puget Sound, Capt. George Vancouver's sloop *Discovery*, was the park's namesake. Hikers will discover nearly 12 miles of trails meandering through forests, open meadows, sand dunes, and sea cliffs. The longest, at 2.8 miles, is the Loop Trail, offering sweeping views of Puget Sound, Alki Point, Vashon, Blakely, and Bainbridge Islands, and the Olympic Mountains.

Distance: 2.8-mile loop

Approximate hiking time: 1.5 to 2 hours

Difficulty: Moderate due to a series of short hills

Trail surface: Packed dirt; paved in a few short stretches

Best season: Year-round

Other trail users: Bicycles and skaters permitted on paved sections only

Canine compatibility: Leashed dogs permitted

Fees and permits: No fees or permits required

Schedule: Open daily, 6:00 a.m. to 11:00 p.m.

Maps: USGS Seattle North W; Seattle street map

Trail contacts: Seattle Parks and Recreation, (206) 684-4075; www.seattle.gov/parks

Finding the trailhead: From downtown Seattle drive west on Denny Way, which becomes Elliott Avenue and eventually 15th Avenue West. Take the Dravus Street exit and turn left at the light onto Dravus Street. Turn right at 20th Avenue West, which becomes Gilman Avenue West and eventually West Government Way. The street ends at the entrance to the park. For easy access to the trail, in the first lot on the left (east parking lot) park inside the park. The trail begins at the information kiosk. GPS: N47 39.50' / W122 24.35'

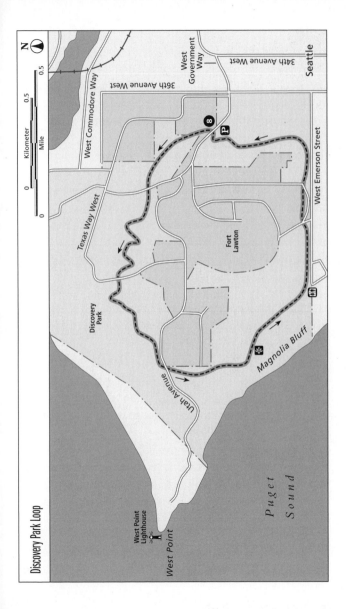

Discovery Park Loop

The Hike

Discovery Park occupies the grounds of Fort Lawton, a former U.S. military base, most of which has been acquired by the city of Seattle for public use. This large park encompasses a variety of terrain, and the well-maintained and heavily traveled Loop Trail passes through them all. This trail is clearly marked at intersections with minor trails and service roads, so if you follow the signs you can't go wrong.

Beginning from the kiosk beside the east parking lot, start walking in a counterclockwise (north) direction. Immediately enter the forest and head up a gentle incline. For much of its length, the trail roller-coasters through a series of easy grades, but the trail is moderately steep (roughly a 10 to 15 percent grade) in a few short spots, so trekking poles can be helpful.

Views throughout most of the hike are limited to the woods, hillsides, ravines, and the creatures that live there, so be on the lookout for bald eagles, great blue herons, woodpeckers, and many other species of birds.

About halfway through the hike, the trail approaches the edge of Magnolia Bluff, a 200-foot sea cliff. Here the expansive eagle's-nest view is breathtaking, and the open terrain of meadow and sand dunes ensures an unobstructed panorama. This is a great spot to linger and take in the ship and ferry traffic below, or simply contemplate the natural beauty of the Puget Sound region. It's tempting to step up to the edge of the bluff, but be sure to observe the warning signs and stay behind the designated area. The bluff is unstable and prone to collapse.

When you're ready to tear yourself away from the view, the trail leads you away from the bluff. The buildings on the hill ahead of you are remnants of the old military base, Fort Lawton Military Reservation, which was instrumental in housing troops in transit during World War II and also served as a POW camp during the war.

The trail heads into the forest again along the south end of the park and soon skirts the right edge of a parking lot (the south lot). Watch for trail markers indicating the Loop Trail and/or the visitor center. They are the same trail and will lead you back to your starting point at the east parking lot trailhead.

Miles and Directions

0.0 Start at the information kiosk near the entrance to the east parking lot and head counterclockwise (north) on the well-marked trail.

1.7 The trail skirts Magnolia Bluff. Be careful to stay away from the edge as you enjoy the views.

2.0 Pass Fort Lawton Military Reservation.

2.3 Skirt the right edge of the south parking lot and look for the Loop Trail/visitor center signs.

2.8 Arrive back at the east parking lot trailhead.

9 Burke-Gilman Trail: Gas Works Park to Fremont

The Burke-Gilman Trail is a heavily traveled multiuse recreational corridor that follows an early railroad route. The entire trail runs more than 18 miles and is part of an extensive network of trails in the region. The portion of the Burke-Gilman Trail between Gas Works Park and Fremont, near the trail's southwest end, offers a glimpse of Seattle's maritime world and striking views of the downtown skyline across Lake Union.

Distance: 2.8 miles out and back
Approximate hiking time: 1.5 hours
Difficulty: Easy, flat trail
Trail surface: Paved
Best season: Year-round
Other trail users: Bicyclists, skaters
Canine compatibility: Leashed dogs permitted
Fees and permits: No fees or permits required
Schedule: Open daily, 4:00 a.m. to 11:30 p.m.
Maps: USGS Seattle North E; Seattle street map
Trail contacts: Seattle Parks and Recreation, (206) 684-4075; www.seattle.gov/parks

Finding the trailhead: From Interstate 5 take exit 169 (Northeast 45th Street) and drive west on Northeast 45th Street. Turn left onto Burke Avenue North and travel until the road ends at North Northlake Way. You will see Gas Works Park across the street. Turn into the park parking lot (four-hour limit). Begin your hike across the street at the base of the Wallingford Steps. The beginning of the trail runs parallel to North Northlake Way. Facing the steps, follow the trail to the left. GPS: N47 38.82' / W122 20.19'

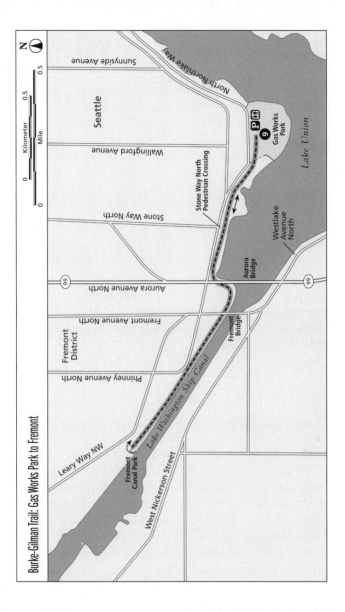

Burke-Gilman Trail: Gas Works Park to Fremont

N

0   Kilometer   0.5

0   Mile   0.5

Seattle

Sunnyside Avenue

North Northlake Way

Wallingford Avenue

Stone Way North Pedestrian Crossing

Stone Way North

Gas Works Park

Lake Union

Westlake Avenue North

P

9

Aurora Bridge

Aurora Avenue North

99

99

Fremont Avenue North

Fremont District

Phinney Avenue North

Leary Way NW

Fremont Canal Park

Lake Washington Ship Canal

Fremont Bridge

West Nickerson Street

The Hike

Gas Works Park, on the north shore of Lake Union, is a Seattle destination in itself. If time allows before you hit the trail, explore the park with its kite hill and the relics of the old gasworks that adorn the picnic and children's play areas. It's a perfect example of how a cleaned-up industrial site can be reclaimed and put to good use. Here, you'll enjoy views of this urban lake flanked by Capitol Hill on one side and Queen Anne Hill on the other, with the downtown skyline straight ahead.

Begin your hike on the paved trail across the street from the park. Facing away from the park, follow the trail to the left (west). Heavily used by bicyclists, the Burke-Gilman Trail is divided into two lanes—one for wheels and the other for feet—but sometimes the line between the lanes fades. Posted signs remind bicyclists that pedestrians have the right-of-way, but it's always a good idea to yield to bikes for your own safety.

The trail passes between a cement retaining wall and a chain-link fence, and here you might be hoping the entire trail isn't this ugly. Be patient. Soon the trail crosses Stone Way North at North 34th Street; continue on between the retaining wall and the Seattle Rowing Club and turn left. The scenery opens up.

Lake Union flows into the Fremont Cut of the Lake Washington Ship Canal. The shore is lined with houseboats (not really boats at all, but floating homes), tugs, sailboats, and fishing trawlers—if it floats, it's here. The imposing Aurora Bridge dominates the sky directly overhead.

The trail passes beneath the Aurora Bridge and then under the smaller, more colorful Fremont Bridge, built in 1916. Brand-name high-tech corporate campuses line the trail as it parallels the canal, continuing west. The trail passes a plaza with natural stone sculptures and another area with ivy dinosaurs and a kiosk with a supply of free *Fremont Walking Tour* brochures.

(Option: If you have time, this is a great place to detour 1 block away from the route and explore the eclectic and artsy Fremont District, which proudly proclaims itself the Center of the Universe.)

When you reach Fremont Canal Park, with its metal grate deck and shelter suspended on the hillside between the trail and the canal, turn around and head back to your starting point at Gas Works Park.

Miles and Directions

0.0 Start at the base of Wallingford Steps on North Northlake Way, across the street from Gas Works Park. There is no trailhead marker. Facing the paved trail with your back to Gas Works Park, begin your hike to the left (west).

0.4 Reach the intersection of Stone Way North and North 34th Street. Cross with the pedestrian traffic light and continue to follow the trail, which parallels North 34th Street behind a cement retaining wall.

0.6 The trail turns left, approaches Lake Union, and crosses under the Aurora Bridge.

0.8 The trail crosses under the Fremont Bridge and continues on, paralleling the Fremont Cut.

1.4 Reach the end of Fremont Canal Park (Northwest Canal Street and Second Avenue NW). Retrace your steps to the trailhead.

2.8 Arrive back at Gas Works Park.

10 Magnuson Park

Warren G. Magnuson Park occupies the site of the former Sand Point Naval Air Station on Lake Washington. When the base was closed, the city of Seattle acquired the land and buildings for public use, making good use of the waterfront and wide-open spaces for recreational and athletic facilities, including miles of trails. (NOTE: As of this writing, large sections of the park were under renovation to restore wetlands and natural habitats as well as improve the athletic fields. Additional hiking trails will be available when the project is completed.)

Distance: 2.6-mile lollipop
Approximate hiking time: 1.5 hours
Difficulty: Easy, with one hill
Trail surface: Paved, gravel
Best season: Year-round
Other trail users: Bicyclists, skaters
Canine compatibility: Leashed dogs permitted; large off-leash area nearby
Fees and permits: No fees or permits required
Schedule: Open year-round; May 1 through Labor Day, 4:00 a.m. to 11:30 p.m.; Labor Day through April 30, 4:00 a.m. to 10:00 p.m.
Maps: USGS Seattle North E and Bellevue North W; Seattle street map
Trail contacts: Seattle Parks and Recreation, (206) 684-4075; www.seattle.gov/parks

Finding the trailhead: From downtown Seattle drive north on Interstate 5 and take exit 169 (Northeast 45th Street). Turn right onto Northeast 45th Street and follow it past the University of Washington and down the hill. The street becomes Sandpoint Way NE and curves to the left. Turn right at Northeast 65th Street, which ends at the Magnuson Park parking lot. The trailhead is to the left of the boat ramp as you face the lake. GPS: N47 40.55' / W122 15.04'

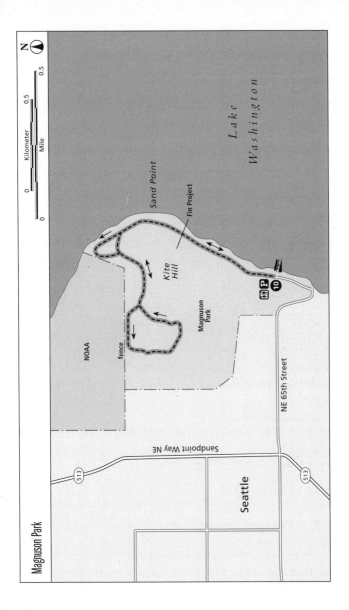

Magnuson Park

The Hike

Lake Washington stretches 20 miles along Seattle's entire eastern border and beyond, its shoreline home to miles of promenades, parks, bicycle trails, waterfront homes, neighborhood commercial districts, a hydroplane racing pit, the on-ramps of two floating bridges, and even the site of a former naval air station. When the Sand Point Naval Air Station closed, the city of Seattle seized the opportunity to acquire the lakefront property to create Magnuson Park, which now shares Sand Point with the National Oceanographic and Atmospheric Administration (NOAA).

Magnuson Park contains miles of trails. This hike follows the lakefront promenade, ascends Sand Point Head (aka Kite Hill), and circles a hilltop field with excellent views up and down the lake, east to the city of Kirkland, and beyond to the Cascade Mountains.

About midway along the promenade, you will notice something resembling killer whale dorsal fins—twenty-two of them in all—breaching the lawn as it gently rolls like waves. These are actually black diving fins from decommissioned Navy attack submarines buried in the hillside, creating a provocative art installation titled *The Fin Project*.

The promenade ends at a gate leading to a high point of the hike for your canine companion, if you brought one: an enormous fenced off-leash area that meanders through the park. This optional delight for your dog will temporarily take you off the trail, but you can backtrack and easily find the gate again and continue up Kite Hill to resume the hike.

A nearby attraction resides on the secured grounds of NOAA: the lakefront Art Walk. One of the highlights of the collection is *Sound Garden,* a collection of pipes that play eerie sounds in the wind, the tone and pitch determined by the wind's direction and velocity. To access Art Walk, go to the NOAA security gate on Northeast 63rd Avenue, immediately to the north of the park, and request access to the Art Walk. If the current security level permits, you will go through a routine security screening, be issued a visitor's pass and permitted to enter.

Miles and Directions

0.0 Start at the lakeside promenade next to the boat launch at the park's south parking lot. Cross the footbridge and follow the promenade north.

0.4 The trail passes *The Fin Project,* an art installation.

0.7 The trail reaches the off-leash area for dogs and turns to the left along the fence.

0.8 At the trail intersection, turn right and follow the trail up Kite Hill and beyond to the athletic fields. Circle the field for great views of the park, and then take the same trail back down the hill.

1.9 Walk straight through the trail intersection toward the lake.

2.0 Turn right at the lakeside promenade and walk south toward the trailhead.

2.6 Arrive back at the trailhead.

11 Sammamish River and Burke-Gilman Trails: Bothell Landing

Bothell Landing, on the north bank of the Sammamish River, is a quaint step back in time. This park contains one of the first pioneer cabins in the area and a collection of later Victorian homes that now house a historical museum and an event space. A footbridge crosses the river to the 11-mile Sammamish River Trail, which hikers can follow in either direction. This hike follows a short segment of the trail along the river to the right.

Distance: 3.4 miles out and back
Approximate hiking time: 1.5 hours
Difficulty: Easy, flat trail with a few gentle inclines
Trail surface: Paved
Best season: Year-round
Other trail users: Bicyclists, skaters
Canine compatibility: Leashed dogs permitted
Fees and permits: No fees or permits required

Schedule: Open year-round; Bothell Landing open 8:00 a.m. to dusk
Maps: USGS Bothell; King County street map
Trail contacts: City of Bothell Parks and Recreation, (425) 486-7430; www.ci.bothell.wa .us/dept/parks/parksindex.html
    King County Parks and Recreation, (206) 296-8687; www .kingcounty.gov/recreation/ parks.aspx

Finding the trailhead: From downtown Seattle drive north on Interstate 5 and take exit 177 (Lake Forest Park). Turn right after the exit and follow Highway 104 to Lake Forest Park. At Lake Forest Park Center, turn left onto Bothell Way NE (Highway 522) and follow it through Kenmore. Turn right at Northeast 180th Street. Drive 1 block and turn right into the Park at Bothell Landing; the trail begins at the footbridge. GPS: N47 45.49' / W122 12.46'

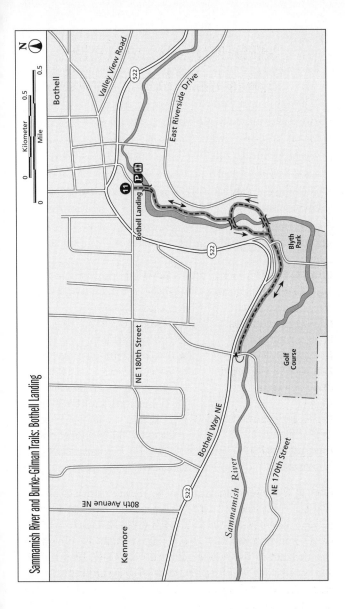

Sammamish River and Burke-Gilman Trails: Bothell Landing

The Hike

The Sammamish River meanders through north King County, flowing from Lake Sammamish to Lake Washington, the two large lakes to the east of Seattle. The trail's 11.0 miles make up a small fraction of the extensive Regional Trail System in King County and can be accessed from many points.

For a perfect short hike, begin at the Park at Bothell Landing, with its collection of historic buildings and nineteenth-century village feel. Take the footbridge across the river and begin your hike to the right. As you enjoy this riverbank trail, keep an eye out for the variety of waterfowl that frequent the river.

The trail follows the south riverbank through woods and grassy slopes, crosses the river again on another footbridge, follows the north bank for a distance, and then divides. This fork marks the end of the Sammamish River Trail and the beginning of the roughly 18-mile Burke-Gilman Trail that heads into Seattle.

The left fork crosses a footbridge to Blyth Park and Norway Hill, where it joins the western trailhead of the 14-mile Tolt Pipeline Trail to the east toward the Cascade foothills. Take the right fork (The Burke-Gilman Trail) and follow it through the underpass and along the easement beside the Wayne Golf Course. This stretch of the trail overlooks the greens, the parklike ground of the course, and the river meandering below.

After the golf course, the trail passes by a riverside residential area on the left and Highway 522 above the retaining wall on the right. As the trail gets closer to the highway, traffic noise and roadside businesses interfere with the countryside ambience of the hike, so this is a good place to turn around and retrace your steps back to Bothell Landing.

Options: You may choose to turn this into a longer hike and continue onward a few more miles through the city of Kenmore to Lake Washington.

On the hike back to Bothell Landing, you may take an alternate route where the Burke-Gilman Trail becomes the Sammamish River Trail (after the underpass). Instead of taking the Sammamish River Trail to the left, take the right fork across the old trestle. As you approach Blyth Park, take the first path on the left (across the trail from the park) paralleling the Sammamish River Trail on the hillside. Turn left at the first junction, a paved trail that rejoins the Sammamish River Trail. Turn right onto the Sammamish River Trail and follow it back to the Park at Bothell Landing.

Miles and Directions

0.0   Start at the Bothell Landing trailhead. Take the footbridge over the river and follow the trail to the right along the river.

0.5   The Sammamish River Trail ends and the Burke-Gilman Trail begins at a fork in the trail. Take the right fork through the underpass on the Burke-Gilman Trail.

1.7   Turn around before you reach Highway 522 and retrace your steps.

2.7   **Option:** For a short alternate route back, take the right fork at the end of the Burke-Gilman Trail, cross the footbridge across the river, and take the first path to the left (across the trail from Blyth Park).

2.9   Turn left at the first trail junction. This paved trail descends the hill and joins the Sammamish River Trail.

3.0   Turn right onto the Sammamish River Trail.

3.4   Arrive back at the trailhead at the Park at Bothell Landing.

12 Soos Creek Trail

The Puget Sound Basin is laced with wetlands, many accessible by excellent, well-maintained trails. Soos Creek is a prime example of a wetland ecosystem in which the creek feeds ponds and swamps and supports a rich diversity of plant and animal life. A multiuse trail extends more than 7 miles one-way beside the creek; this hike explores the northern segment of that trail.

Distance: 5.0 miles out and back

Approximate hiking time: 2 to 2.5 hours

Difficulty: Moderate due to distance and a few gradual inclines

Trail surface: Paved

Best season: Year-round

Other trail users: Bicyclists, skaters, equestrians (on the soft surface shoulder and parallel horse trail)

Canine compatibility: Leashed dogs permitted

Fees and permits: No fees or permits required

Schedule: Open-year round, dawn to dusk

Maps: USGS Renton, WA; South King County street map

Trail contacts: King County Parks and Recreation, (206) 296-8687; www.kingcounty.gov/recreation/parks.aspx

Finding the trailhead: From Seattle drive south on Interstate 5. Take exit 152 (South 188th Street/Orillia Road South) and turn left onto South 188th Street, which immediately curves right onto Orillia Road South. Follow Orillia Road South down the hill; the road curves left and become South 212th Street. Follow this street through the valley, under the Highway 167 overpass, and up the hill where it becomes Southeast 208th Street. Turn left into the signed parking lot at Soos Creek Park. GPS (north trailhead): N47 24.97' / W122 9.56'

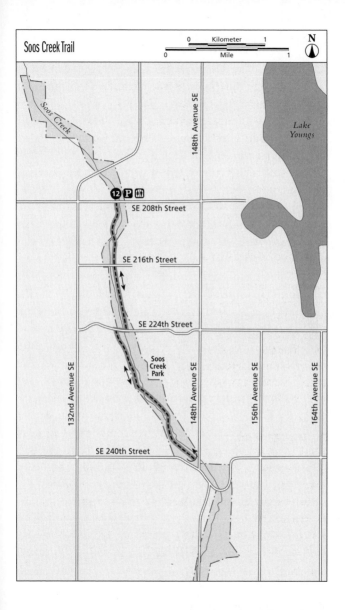

Soos Creek Trail

0   Kilometer   1

0   Mile   1

N

Soos Creek

148th Avenue SE

Lake
Youngs

12 P 🚻

SE 208th Street

SE 216th Street

SE 224th Street

132nd Avenue SE

Soos
Creek
Park

148th Avenue SE

156th Avenue SE

164th Avenue SE

SE 240th Street

The Hike

A long stretch of Soos Creek—an important tributary of the Duwamish and Green River Watershed—is bordered by a wide greenbelt of wetlands that has been set aside as a county park with a paved multiuse trail. This trail offers an excellent opportunity to explore a natural wetland environment without traveling far from the city.

The trail begins at Soos Creek Park, which has parking, restrooms, a picnic shelter, and a children's play area. A short spur of the Soos Creek Trail heads north through the park and dead-ends in 0.5 mile. Instead, for a longer hike through the wetlands, cross the street and the footbridge and head south on the paved trail.

At first the trail cuts a path close to pastures and stables, but soon the wetlands expand and the landscape is rich with cattails, alders, and other wetland vegetation above the surface of the water and plants such as water parsley below. The branches here are heavy with moss, and opportunistic ferns set down roots wherever they can. This trail is popular with birders for a reason; watch for waterfowl, hawks, and other birds that make the wetlands their home.

At the 0.5-mile point, the trail crosses a street. At 1.0 mile a country road interrupts the trail, but the trail resumes across the road about 450 feet to the right. Here the trail follows some power lines for about 0.25 mile but never leaves the wetlands. The trail then heads up and down a few gentle slopes as it enters a riparian forest that overlooks the creek below.

You eventually hear but not see evidence of civilization again, with the roar of a highway just up the ridge. When you come to the next road, you can turn around and retrace your steps back to the trailhead to complete the 5.0-mile round-trip hike or cross the road and continue on to add more mileage.

Miles and Directions

0.0 Start at the north trailhead, across the street from the park. Cross the street and continue south across the footbridge.

0.5 The trail crosses another street.

1.0 Come to a rural road. Turn right onto the road, walk 450 feet, and turn left onto the trail, which is well marked.

2.5 Turnaround and retrace your steps back to the trailhead. **Option:** For a longer hike—more than twice the length, round trip—continue on to the south end of the trail, where you will turn around and return to the north trailhead.

5.0 Arrive back at the north trailhead.

13 Mercer Slough Nature Park

The largest wetlands on the shores of Lake Washington have been preserved as Mercer Slough Nature Park. The park's well-maintained interpretive trails provide easy access to this important wildlife habitat. Day hikers not only enjoy the outdoors but also learn about wetland wildlife, the fascinating history of the area's early settlers, and the only operating blueberry farm in the vicinity, which thrives in the boggy wetland soil.

Distance: 2.1-mile double loop

Approximate hiking time: 1 hour

Difficulty: Easy, flat trail

Trail surface: Raised boardwalk, bark chips, dirt

Best season: Year-round

Other trail users: None

Canine compatibility: Leashed dogs permitted

Fees and permits: No fees or permits required

Schedule: Open year-round, dawn to dusk

Maps: USGS Bellevue South W; Bellevue street map

Trail contacts: Bellevue Parks, (425) 452-6885; www.ci .bellevue.wa.us/parks_home page.htm

Finding the trailhead: From Seattle drive east on Interstate 90, and take exit 9 (Bellevue Way SE). Drive north on Bellevue Way SE and watch for the WINTERS HOUSE sign on the right. Turn right into the parking lot. The trailhead begins behind the Winters House. GPS: N47 35.49' / W122 11.58'

The Hike

In 1856 Native American tribes assembled at a place called *sa'tsakal* to organize an assault on the pioneer settlement

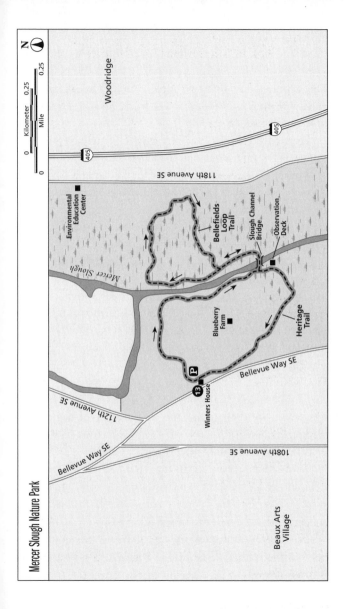

Mercer Slough Nature Park

of Seattle. That staging ground was located at present-day Mercer Slough, and the skirmish, a failed protest over treaty terms, would later become known as the Battle of Seattle. Today the city of Bellevue surrounds Mercer Slough and the vast natural wetlands that border it, a habitat for more than 170 species of wildlife.

Start your hike on the Heritage Trail behind Winters House. This trail begins on a long raised boardwalk over the bogs and wetlands and eventually becomes a bark-chip trail following the edge of a working blueberry farm. The trail soon reaches the slough and crosses the Slough Channel Bridge—a footbridge that's a great place to pause and see how many species of waterfowl you can spot.

On the other side of the slough, the Bellefields Loop Trail begins on the left and switches between a boardwalk and soft-surface trail with wetland interpretive displays along the route. Follow this trail to the left for a clockwise hike through wetlands, into an upland forest, down through wetlands again, and back to the Slough Channel Bridge. A few unmarked trail junctions can make the Bellefields Loop Trail confusing, but if you remember that when in doubt you should follow the right-hand fork for a clockwise loop, you won't go wrong. The only exception is at the end of the loop, where a left-hand turn onto the raised boardwalk leads you back to the Slough Channel Bridge.

Across the bridge, rejoin the Heritage Trail. Immediately on the left, a short spur to a viewing deck provides a quiet spot to rest and observe wetland life. As you continue on the Heritage Trail, the modern high-rises of downtown Bellevue come into view on one side and the summit of Mt. Rainier on the other. Follow the trail signs back to the Winters House.

The Mercer Slough Environmental Education Center, not on this hike's route, is located across the park at the 118th Avenue SE entrance. Great for kids and adults, the center's worth a visit for the interpretive displays about the wetlands and local history, nature art exhibits, and educational programs. A quick visit to the center prior to hitting the trail can make your hike through Mercer Slough Nature Park a more informed experience.

Miles and Directions

0.0 Start at the trailhead behind the Winters House.

0.5 Turn left at the trail intersection, cross the Slough Channel Bridge (footbridge), and follow the raised boardwalk to the left (Bellefields Trail).

0.7 The trail forks; follow the left fork for a clockwise loop on the Bellefields Trail.

1.0 Come to an unsigned junction. Follow the trail on the right.

1.1 Come to another unsigned junction. Follow the trail on the right.

1.3 At the trail junction, follow the trail on the right directing you to Slough Channel Bridge.

1.4 At the trail junction, turn left and follow the trail on the raised boardwalk.

1.5 Cross the Slough Channel Bridge and turn left for a short spur trail to an observation platform. Back at the main trail, turn left.

1.6 At the trail junction, turn right and follow the trail back to Winters House and the trailhead.

2.1 Arrive back at the trailhead.

14 Cougar Mountain Regional Wildland Park: Red Town and Wildside Trails

Cougar Mountain stands as the westernmost of the Issaquah Alps, what remains of a mountain range that geologically predates the nearby Cascades. With more than 3,000 acres and 36 miles of hiking trails at all levels of difficulty, Cougar Mountain Regional Wildland Park reigns as the king of King County Parks.

Distance: 1.7-mile loop

Approximate hiking time: 1 to 1.5 hours

Difficulty: Moderate due to several short hills with more than a 100-foot elevation gain

Trail surface: Dirt and gravel

Best season: Year-round; but trails muddy after a rain

Other trail users: Equestrians on portions of the trail

Canine compatibility: Leashed dogs permitted

Fees and permits: No fees or permits required

Schedule: Open year round, 8:00 a.m. to dusk

Maps: USGS Issaquah; King Co. street map

Trail contacts: King County Parks and Recreation, (206) 296-8687; www.kingcounty.gov/recreation/parks.aspx

Finding the trailhead: From Seattle drive east on Interstate 90 and take exit 13 (Lakemont Boulevard SE). Follow Lakemont Boulevard SE until you come to a sign on the left for the Red Town Trail. Turn into the parking lot. All the trails in the park are well signed. GPS: N47 32.09' / W122 7.74'

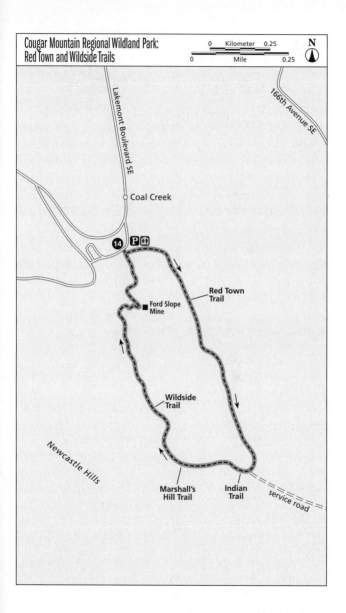

Cougar Mountain Regional Wildland Park:
Red Town and Wildside Trails

Kilometer
0
0.25

Mile
0
0.25

N

166th Avenue SE

Lakemont Boulevard SE

Coal Creek

14 P

Red Town
Trail

Ford Slope
Mine

Wildside
Trail

Newcastle Hills

Marshall's
Hill Trail

Indian
Trail

service road

The Hike

The Seattle region's coal mining past largely lies hidden beneath the forest floor on the western slopes of Cougar Mountain. If it weren't for a few preserved artifacts and interpretive kiosks, hikers on the mountain's trails would remain clueless that less than a hundred years ago, a vast coal mining operation and a community of miners and their families—Red Town, a neighborhood of nearby Newcastle—occupied the mountainside where lush forest now stands. In less than a century, nature has completely reclaimed the mountain.

Red Town Trail, basically a gravel-and-dirt service road, leaves the parking lot on a gradual ascent. Hikers pass the junction to the more difficult Cave Hole Trail and several smaller spur trails, perhaps considerations for future hiking trips to this large, close-to-civilization park. Red Town Trail eventually narrows and becomes Indian Trail at a junction with an optional side path that passes a meadow restoration project with information posted about the project and the history of Red Town.

To complete the loop, transfer to Marshall's Hill Trail and then, after a short distance, to Wildside Trail, which winds and rolls gently through the thick forest.

Near the end of the loop, a short spur leads to Ford Slope Mine, where you will see the sealed entrance to the coal mine with a rusty air vent still protruding from the ground. A nearby steam hoist—its foundation still in the forest—lowered the miners more than 1,700 feet into the mine shaft, which bottoms out 200 feet below sea level, and hauled the coal out. An excellent kiosk display of historic photos of miners waiting to be lowered into the mine at the very spot where you are standing breathes life into the site. Other captioned photos of the mining operation, the town, and the miners and their families round out the experience.

When hiking Cougar Mountain, trekking poles are useful to help negotiate the few slopes and the slippery trail surfaces after a rain. Although the park's trails are well signed, due to the number of trails and trail junctions, a park map available online or at the trailhead kiosk can come in handy. Also, it is crucial to stay on the trails. The former mining operation scarred Cougar Mountain with possible hazards, such as unstable ground, the potential of collapsing mineshafts, and hidden mining hardware.

Miles and Directions

0.0 Start at the parking lot and begin walking on the Red Town Trail, a wide gravel-and-dirt service road to the left of the kiosk. Follow the road up the hill.

0.8 Red Town Trail ends and becomes Indian Trail. (**Option:** At this signed junction an alternate trail goes past the Meadow Restoration Project and joins the main trail again in a short distance.) Just past the Indian trailhead, come to another signed junction. Leave Indian Trail and follow Marshall's Hill Trail straight ahead.

1.0 Walk through the wooden equestrian barrier and straight ahead onto the Wildside Trail.

1.5 Follow the short spur to Ford Slope Mine, where you will find historic information and mining relics.

1.7 Arrive back at the trailhead.

15 Squak Mountain

Squak Mountain has been preserved as a vast, wooded state park that's just minutes from Seattle. Its trails range from easy to difficult, but all have one thing in common: They share a quintessential Pacific Northwest forest that's closed to all activity except hiking, running, and, on designated trails, horseback riding (so watch your step).

Distance: 3.4-mile lollipop
Approximate hiking time: 2.5 hours
Difficulty: More challenging due to a 700-foot elevation gain and loss
Trail surface: Dirt and gravel
Best season: Year-round
Other trail users: Equestrians on segments of the trail
Canine compatibility: Leashed dogs permitted

Fees and permits: No fees or permits required
Schedule: Open year-round; summer hours, 6:30 a.m. to dusk; winter hours, 8:00 a.m. to dusk
Maps: USGS Maple Valley; King County street map
Trail contacts: Washington State Parks, (360) 902-8844; www.parks.wa.gov

Finding the trailhead: From Interstate 90 take exit 15 and follow Highway 900 south. Turn left onto Southeast May Valley Road and turn left into Squak Mountain State Park. The trailhead is on the left side of the parking lot. GPS: N47 28.90' / W122 3.26'

The Hike

The Issaquah Alps have many outstanding features that rank them among the best recreational assets in the Seattle area. One of those is their close proximity to the city. Squak Mountain, the "alp" between Cougar and Tiger Mountains

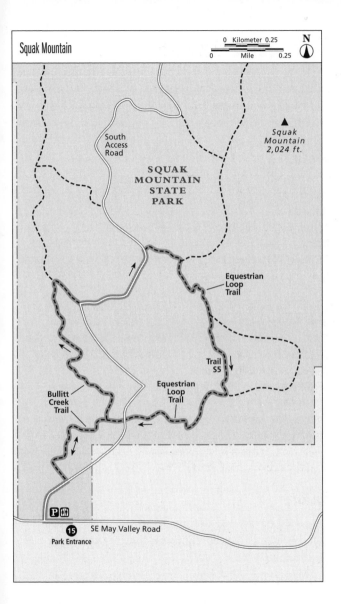

Squak Mountain

0   Kilometer   0.25

0   Mile   0.25

N

South
Access
Road

SQUAK
MOUNTAIN
STATE
PARK

▲
*Squak
Mountain*
2,024 ft.

Equestrian
Loop
Trail

Trail
S5

Bullitt
Creek
Trail

Equestrian
Loop
Trail

P ♿

15
Park Entrance

SE May Valley Road

contains a network of trails crisscrossing the heavily wooded hillsides. The trails can be muddy and some have moderately steep stretches, so trekking poles are a good idea.

Although the Squak Mountain route described here, which explores the south flank of the mountain, has an approximate 700-foot elevation gain and loss, it was selected for this guide to allow hikers to experience the park's natural environment without excessive uphill hiking. The lasso-shaped route begins at the south trailhead at the parking lot and loops clockwise uphill on the lower portion of the Bullitt Creek Trail, up a portion of the South Access Road (closed to motorized public traffic) and down the Equestrian Loop Trail, with a few connector and shortcut trails in between.

A short distance past the trailhead, an optional, flat 0.3-mile interpretive nature trail loops through the forest. To the right of the nature trail, the Bullitt Creek Trail—the beginning of your route—begins.

Squak Mountain's story, like so many in the Pacific Northwest, is one of stewardship and conservation. Until the mid-twentieth century, Squak Mountain was heavily logged and mined. A prominent Seattle family rescued the mountain from commercial enterprise and donated the land to the state with the proviso that it be allowed to return to its natural state. Today visitors to Squak Mountain State Park have to look hard to find any reminders of the mountain's commercial past. Nature has reclaimed the mountain with a vengeance. The trails meander up and down through moss- and fern-laden forest, through thickly wooded ravines, and beside and over cascading creeks and waterfalls. You won't find sweeping vistas on this route, but you will find a quiet, meditative forest.

Since some Squak Mountain trail junctions are unmarked,

it's easy to get lost or inadvertently extend your hike. An excellent supplement to the map provided with this hike is the trail map available at the trailhead kiosk. With a park map you can follow the route described here or create your own. If you create your own route, be mindful of distance and elevation gain.

Miles and Directions

0.0 Start at the trailhead at the Squak Mountain State park parking lot.

0.1 The trail crosses South Access Road and resumes to the right of the nature trail. On the state park trail map, this is identified as the Bullitt Creek Trail.

0.5 Come to a junction and follow the left fork to remain on the Bullitt Creek Trail.

1.0 At the junction, follow the right fork, leaving the Bullitt Creek Trail.

1.2 The trail joins the South Access Road; turn left and follow the road up the hill.

1.5 The Equestrian Loop Trail intersects the road on the right; turn right onto the trail.

1.6 At the junction, turn right to remain on the Equestrian Loop Trail and follow it down the hill.

2.3 At an easy-to-miss junction, marked as Trail S5, turn right onto S5, a shortcut that leaves and rejoins the main trail. If you miss the junction and remain on the Equestrian Loop Trail, you will simply extend your hike.

2.5 Trail S5 ends at the Equestrian Loop Trail. Turn right and follow it down the ravine, across the footbridge, and up the hill, where it will eventually cross the South Access Road and continue on.

2.9 The trail forks; follow the left fork onto the Bullitt Creek Trail.

3.4 Arrive back at the trailhead and parking lot.

16 Tiger Mountain: Around the Lake Trail

When it comes to a hiking destination, what could be more satisfying than 14,000 acres of heavily forested mountain with 70 miles of hiking trails only thirty minutes from downtown Seattle? That's right . . . nothing. Tiger Mountain serves up a sumptuous spread for the hungry hiker, offering everything from easy nature trails to long, steep terrain. The Around the Lake Trail, which circles Tradition Lake, provides an easy and accessible introduction to Tiger Mountain.

Distance: 1.5-mile loop
Approximate hiking time: 1 hour
Difficulty: Easy, flat trail
Trail surface: Dirt
Best season: Year-round, but winter snow and ice conditions can prevent access or make the hike more challenging
Other trail users: None
Canine compatibility: Leashed dogs permitted

Fees and permits: No fees or permits required
Schedule: Open year-round, dawn to dusk; parking lot gate locked at dusk
Maps: USGS Issaquah and Fall City; King County street map
Trail contacts: State of Washington Department of Natural Resources, (360) 902-1000; www.dnr.wa.gov

Finding the trailhead: From Seattle drive east on Interstate 90 and take exit 20 (High Point). After the exit, turn right and then take another immediate right onto Southeast 79th Street. The trailhead parking lot is at the end of the road. If the gate is closed or the lot is full, park along Southeast 79th Street at the bottom of the hill and walk approximately 0.25 mile up to the parking lot. GPS: N47 31.78' / W121 59.74'

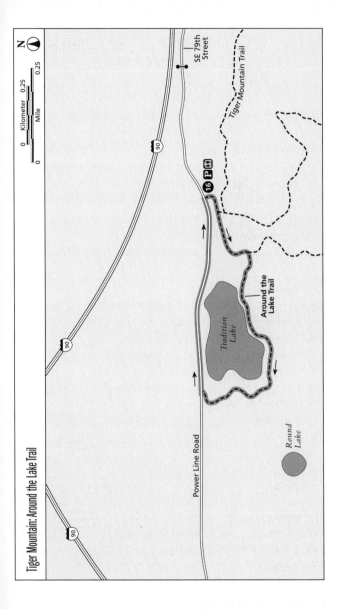

Tiger Mountain: Around the Lake Trail

SE 79th Street

Tiger Mountain Trail

90

16 P

Around the
Lake Trail

Tradition
Lake

90

Power Line Road

90

Round
Lake

N

0   Kilometer   0.25
0   Mile   0.25

The Hike

The third in the series of Issaquah Alps heading east from Seattle is Tiger Mountain. And, like its nearby companions, it was heavily exploited during the Northwest logging boom. A 1910 sawmill and the second-longest incline railroad in the United States, used to transport the logs down the ridges to the mill, once dominated the mountain.

Although Tiger Mountain is used heavily today for recreation, it is not a park. Tiger Mountain State Forest is an experimental forest where water and air quality management, wildlife and fish habitat, timber operations, and recreation coexist. The northwest side of Tiger Mountain, the site of the route described here, has been designated as the West Tiger Mountain Natural Resources Conservation Area. Logging is prohibited, and preservation of the environment and natural habitat is the top land-management priority, even over recreational use.

Tradition Lake sits on a forested plateau on the other side of a low ridge from I-90, which acts as an effective barrier against traffic noise. The Around the Lake Trail is a short, flat loop that circles the lake a respectable distance from the shore, allowing wildlife undisturbed access to the lake. The trail winds through second-growth forest, lush undergrowth, and some giant Douglas firs that early loggers must have spared. Viewing platforms and benches near the lake, designed to give both humans and wildlife their respective spaces, provide plenty of spots to pause and observe the lake. Signs along the trail identify various animal tracks, a fun feature for kids. The trail joins a power-line access road, closed to public traffic, which follows the north side of the lake and rejoins the trail.

If you have more time for a longer hike, the High Point trailhead is the starting point for many trails in the West Tiger Mountain Natural Resources Conservation Area. Be aware of elevation gain and distance before you set out on an alternative hike. Although Tiger Mountain trails tend to be well signed, a trail map can come in handy.

Miles and Directions

0.0 Start at the trailhead beside the parking lot near the restrooms. A trail map sign marks the trailhead. (FYI: A gated road allows vehicle access to the High Point trailhead parking lot. If the gate is closed, park on the road outside the gate and walk up to the parking lot.)

0.1 At the trail junction, turn right to follow the signed Around the Lake Trail.

0.5 At the trail junction, turn right to follow the signed Around the Lake Trail.

0.8 Turn right onto Power Line Road.

1.4 Turn right onto the signed trail to follow the Around the Lake Trail back to the trailhead.

1.5 Arrive back at the trailhead.

17 Preston-Snoqualmie Trail: Lake Alice to Snoqualmie Falls Overlook

The historic Preston-Snoqualmie Trail crosses the foothills above the Raging River Valley, a 6.5-mile trail that is a part of the much larger network of King County Regional Trails. This short hike takes in the most scenic portion of the trail—the last few miles at its eastern end. What's so scenic? The trail terminates at a viewpoint that looks across the valley to 268-foot-high Snoqualmie Falls.

Distance: 3.7 miles out and back

Approximate hiking time: 1.5 to 2 hours

Difficulty: Easy, flat trail with one gentle incline

Trail surface: Paved

Best season: Year-round; the winter rainy season adds volume to the falls.

Other trail users: Bicyclists, skaters

Canine compatibility: Leashed dogs permitted

Fees and permits: No fees or permits required

Schedule: Open year-round, dawn to dusk

Maps: USGS Fall City and USGS Snoqualmie; King County street map

Trail contacts: King County Parks and Recreation, (206) 296-8687; www.kingcounty.gov/recreation/parks.aspx

Finding the trailhead: From Seattle drive east on Interstate 90 and take exit 22. Turn left and drive over the overpass. Turn right at the first intersection and drive through Preston. The road becomes Preston–Fall City Road SE. Turn right onto Southeast 47th Street and then right onto Lake Alice Road. Drive up the hill until you reach the well-signed trailhead and turn right into the parking lot. GPS: N47 33.05' / W121 53.23'

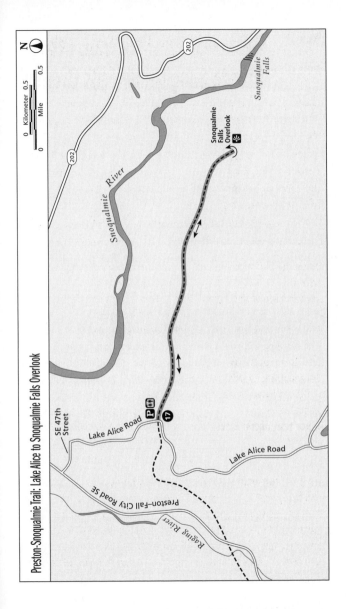

Preston-Snoqualmie Trail: Lake Alice to Snoqualmie Falls Overlook

N

0   Kilometer   0.5
0   Mile   0.5

202

Snoqualmie River

202

Snoqualmie Falls

Snoqualmie Falls Overlook

SE 47th Street

Lake Alice Road

Lake Alice Road

Preston–Fall City Road SE

Raging River

P

17

The Hike

Snoqualmie Falls is the site of the region's first hydroelectric plant, built in 1898. Still in operation, the plant provides the Seattle metropolitan area with much of its power.

Nearly 100 feet higher than Niagara Falls, Snoqualmie Falls drop from a height of 268 feet; the width varies based on the time of year and the amount of rainfall. The site of the falls attracts 1.5 million visitors a year, but from the Preston-Snoqualmie Trail, you're likely to have the view of the falls all to yourself.

This paved, straight, gradually graded trail begins in a residential area in rural King County, but soon the residential properties thin out and the trail follows the side of wooded Snoqualmie Ridge high above the Raging River and Snoqualmie River valleys. In spite of the trail's proximity to civilization, a sign at the trailhead with graphics of a bear and cougar remind you that you are treading in wildlife habitat.

The trail follows a historic railroad grade (as do many of the region's trails) that played a major role in populating the fertile valleys at the foot of the Cascades as well as transporting timber and coal. Today there's no visible evidence of the area's timber and railroad history along this portion of the Preston-Snoqualmie Trail.

History buffs will enjoy a separate visit to the trail's nearby namesake towns: the historic sawmill town of Preston and the railroad town of Snoqualmie, home to the Northwest Railroad Museum, with its period depot and impressive collection of vintage railroad cars lining the main street.

If treading in a place that had a hand in shaping the region's history doesn't entice you, the view at the end of the trail surely will: the long drop of Snoqualmie Falls, the visitor center and lodge perched at the top of the falls, and the jagged Cascade peaks rising above it all.

Miles and Directions

0.0 Start at the trailhead, which is across Lake Alice Road from the parking lot.

0.5 The trail gradually descends into a shallow ravine and out again.

0.7 The trail passes a viewpoint with benches overlooking the Snoqualmie Valley.

1.8 The trail dead-ends at the Snoqualmie Falls overlook. Retrace your steps.

3.7 Arrive back at the trailhead.

18 Twin Falls Trail

Some hikes are extraordinary for the beauty of the terrain they cross and some for the reward at the end of the trail. The Twin Falls Trail is extraordinary for both. The trail follows the South Fork of the Snoqualmie, passes through old-growth forest, and reaches two breathtaking waterfalls, one above the other.

Distance: 2.5 miles out and back
Approximate hiking time: 2 hours
Difficulty: More challenging due to switchbacks and a net elevation gain and loss of approximately 500 feet
Trail surface: Dirt, wooden footbridge
Best season: Spring through fall; winter snow and ice can make the trail inaccessible or at least difficult.

Other trail users: None
Canine compatibility: Leashed dogs permitted
Fees and permits: No fees or permits required
Schedule: Open year-round; 8:00 a.m. to dusk
Maps: USGS Chester Morse Lake; King County street map
Trail contacts: Washington State Parks, (360) 902-8844; www.parks.wa.gov

Finding the trailhead: From Seattle drive east on Interstate 90 and take exit 34. Turn right onto 468th Street SE and turn left onto Southeast 159th. The road ends at the trailhead parking lot. GPS: N47 27.18' / W121 42.34'

The Hike

Twin Falls is accessible from two trailheads, one above the falls and one below. Both are within the boundaries of Olal-

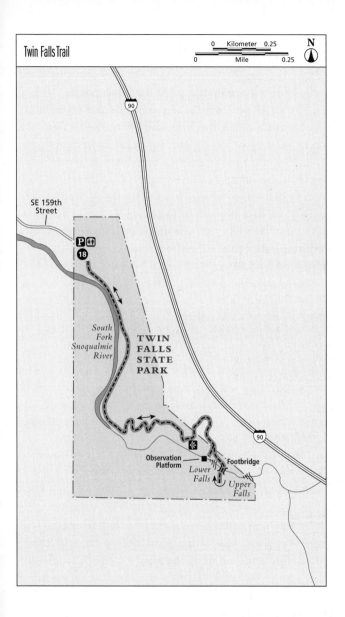

lie State Park, although the lower trailhead has signs indicating it is Twin Falls State Park. According to the Washington State Park map, the lower trailhead and falls are within the Twin Falls Natural Area, a portion of Olallie State Park.

The route described here starts at the lower trailhead, which begins along the bank of the rushing Snoqualmie River, its icy waters fresh from the peaks above Snoqualmie Pass. The trail winds its way through a grove of giant maples, their trunks and branches thickly coated with pads of moss and spiked with ferns, making this spot an oasis of green even in winter. The maples give way to remnants of old-growth forest, the star of which is the "Grandfather Tree," a giant Douglas fir, 14-feet in diameter, that's estimated to be about 700 years old.

About two-thirds of the distance to the falls, you come to benches that have been installed on a ridge, a perfect spot to catch your breath and take in the view of the falls and your ultimate destination across the canyon. Farther on, just before the falls, a stairway spurs off the main trail and leads 103 steps down to a railed wooden viewing platform perched over the edge of the gorge—directly in the face of the 135-foot lower falls. Look straight down into the jade pools, where over time the force of constantly pounding water has carved a cave into the rock. In winter the volume of water in the falls increases significantly, making the sight all the more spectacular.

When you reach the upper falls, an 80-foot-long footbridge crosses the gorge between the two waterfalls. The upper falls tumble down the rocks as though over giant stair steps; the lower falls form a straight drop-off below you. The bridge is a good turnaround point.

If you want to extend the hike, continue on past the bridge to join the Iron Horse Trail at the Upper Twin Falls trailhead.

Miles and Directions

0.0   Start at the signed trailhead at the end of the parking lot.

0.7   Come to a rest area with benches overlooking the waterfall.

1.1   An optional spur with 103 steps leads approximately 200 feet down to a viewing platform is well worth the climb for the close-up view of the lower falls.

1.2   Reach a footbridge spanning the gorge between the upper and lower falls. Turn around on the bridge and retrace your steps back to the trailhead.

2.5   Arrive back at the trailhead.

19 Iron Horse Trail: Upper Twin Falls to Mine Creek

One of the greatest challenges of early railroad construction in Washington was cutting a route through the rugged Cascades, but the Chicago-Milwaukee–St. Paul–Pacific Railroad achieved this with its historic route across Snoqualmie Pass. Today more than 100 miles of that route have become Iron Horse State Park, with its trail following the old railroad grade. This hike goes through deep forest and crosses high trestles with breathtaking views as it skirts the steep northern flank of Mt. Washington.

Distance: 5.6 miles out and back

Approximate hiking time: 2.5 to 3 hours

Difficulty: Moderate due to distance and a sloped access road

Trail surface: Dirt, ballast

Best season: Year-round, but be prepared for snow and ice in winter

Other trail users: Bicyclists, equestrians

Canine compatibility: Leashed dogs permitted

Fees and permits: No fees or permits required

Schedule: Open year-round; summer hours 6:30 a.m. to 9:00 p.m.; winter hours 8:00 a.m. to 5:00 p.m.

Maps: USGS Chester Morse Lake; Washington state road map

Trail contacts: Washington State Parks, (360) 902-8844; www.parks.wa.gov

Finding the trailhead: From Seattle drive east on Interstate 90 and take exit 38 (Olallie State Park). After the exit turn right onto Southeast Homestead Valley Road. Take the first right at the sign to Upper Twin Falls. The road ends in a short distance at the parking lot. GPS: N47 26.50' / W121 40.25'

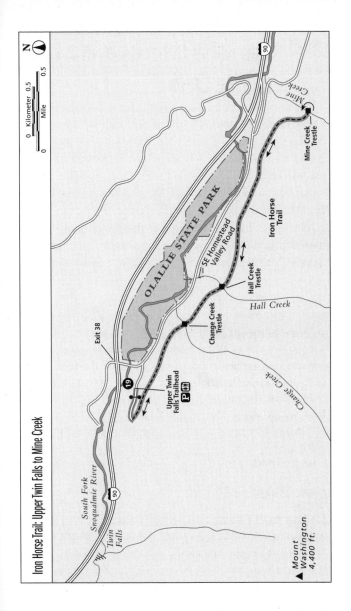

Iron Horse Trail: Upper Twin Falls to Mine Creek

N

0   Kilometer   0.5

0   Mile   0.5

South Fork
Snoqualmie River

Twin
Falls

90

OLALLIE STATE PARK

Exit 38

19

Upper Twin
Falls Trailhead
P

Change Creek
Trestle

Change Creek

Hall Creek
Trestle

Hall Creek

SE Homestead
Valley Road

Iron Horse
Trail

Mine Creek
Trestle

Mine Creek

90

▲ Mount
Washington
4,400 ft.

The Hike

The more than 100-mile Iron Horse Trail offers plenty of segments that are perfect for easy day hiking. The route described here includes a section of the trail's western portion about forty minutes from Seattle.

The service road that you must climb above the Upper Twin Falls parking lot to reach the Iron Horse Trail dead-ends at the trail. (There is no sign indicating that you've reached the Iron Horse Trail.) The trail runs to the left and the right. Follow the trail left (eastbound).

The rugged, steep terrain of Mt. Washington towers above the trail on the right. Below, on the left, the Snoqualmie River rushes through the valley, obscured by the terrain. The trail follows a barely noticeable grade up the old railroad bed and passes the Deception Crags rock-climbing area popular with experienced climbers. At first the traffic noise from I-90 in the valley below competes with the peace and quiet of this mountain trail, but the trail curves away from the freeway, and soon the noise diminishes and then vanishes altogether.

One of the most exhilarating aspects of this hike, the railroad trestles—three of them—offer thrilling views straight down into rugged ravines and canyons, with creeks and waterfalls cascading down the face of Mt. Washington. The first trestle crosses Change Creek, the second Hall Creek (misspelled as Hull Creek on the trail sign), and the third Mine Creek. All three trestles have been outfitted for safety with solid trailbeds filled with ballast and high railings protected with child- and canine-proof chain-link fencing.

The Iron Horse Trail gets heavy use in spring, summer, and fall, and it's no wonder. A gentle grade in rugged mountain terrain on a historic railroad bed complete with breathtaking trestles is difficult for any hiker to resist. In winter the trail sees sparser use. Snow and ice render the hike more challenging, but trekking poles and waterproof boots with good tread can make this trail a pleasure in winter—a time when the creeks and waterfalls cascading below the trestles will likely be flowing to full capacity in a spectacular show.

Miles and Directions

0.0   Start from the Upper Twin Falls parking lot in Olallie State Park. Walk past the barricade and up the gravel service road.

0.2   The road intersects the unmarked Iron Horse Trail. Turn left (east) and follow the trail.

0.8   The Trail passes the Deception Crags rock-climbing area.

1.0   Cross Change Creek Trestle.

1.4   Cross Hall Creek Trestle.

2.8   The trail reaches Mine Creek Trestle. Retrace your steps back to the trailhead. **Option:** Continue on, following the Iron Horse Trail for as long as you like. If you extend the hike, pay attention to the distance and time of day. Since this is an out-and-back trail, your mileage and time on the trail will double on the return trip.

5.4   Turn right onto the access road.

5.6   Arrive back at the trailhead and parking lot.

20 Asahel Curtis Nature Trail

Early photographer Asahel Curtis had a passion for documenting the world around him, including the beauty of the Northwest outdoors. With logging, mining, and the influx of settlers around the turn of the twentieth century, the Northwest was about to change forever, and Curtis's work chronicled that historic shift. It seems fitting then that a nature trail through one of the last remaining old-growth forests only an hour from Seattle should be given his name.

Distance: 1.3-mile lollipop
Approximate hiking time: 1 hour
Difficulty: Easy trail with 100-foot elevation gain and loss
Trail surface: Dirt, gravel, plank boardwalk
Best season: May through November
Other trail users: None
Canine compatibility: Leashed dogs permitted
Fees and permits: Northwest Forest Pass required; for informa-tion on purchasing a pass, see "Trail contacts" below.
Schedule: Open spring through fall, dawn to dusk; closed in winter
Maps: USGS Snoqualmie Pass; Washington state road map
Trail contacts: USDA Forest Service, Mt. Baker–Snoqualmie National Forest, (206) 470-4060 (outdoor recreation information); www.fs.fed.us/r6/mbs

Finding the trailhead: From Seattle drive east on Interstate 90 and take exit 47. Turn right, cross the bridge, and take the first left, which leads to the parking lot. Or simply follow the signs from the freeway to the Asahel Curtis Nature Trail. GPS: N47 23.57' / W121 28.50'

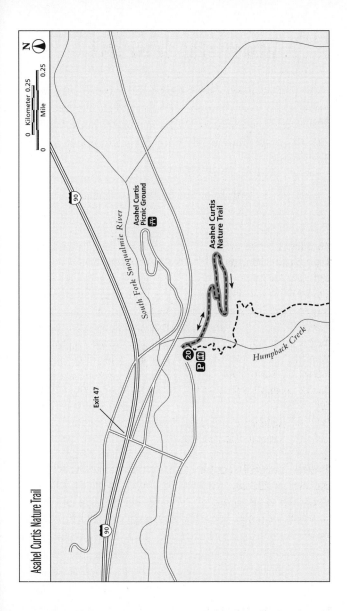

Asahel Curtis Nature Trail

N

0 Kilometer 0.25
0 Mile 0.25

90

South Fork Snoqualmie River

Asahel Curtis Picnic Ground

Asahel Curtis Nature Trail

20
P

Humpback Creek

Exit 47

90

The Hike

Asahel Curtis was a renowned photographer and 1906 cofounder of the Mountaineers Club. To hike the Asahel Curtis Nature Trail is literally to feel dwarfed by raw nature. Douglas fir, western hemlock, and western red cedar are among the giants still thriving there, some rising roughly 200 feet.

The trail sits just off I-90, making it very accessible and easy to find. Unfortunately, the freeway noise is a presence, but it's one that's easily disregarded as you begin to marvel at this ancient forest.

Pick up an interpretive brochure at the trailhead before you begin the hike. This excellent interpretive trail highlights many of the features characteristic of Pacific Northwest forests, such as nurse logs—fallen trees that become seeding ground for anything that can sprout roots or produce spores—and various native plants and trees. In spring and summer the forest floor comes alive with wildflowers—trillium, bleeding heart, wild ginger, orchids, and more.

The first part of the trail follows Humpback Creek as it tumbles and rushes through the dense forest. Sturdy log and plank bridges cross the creek several times as it hurries to become part of the Snoqualmie River. The trail gradually gains a bit of elevation as it enters the old-growth forest and eventually gives way to a marshy wetland accessible over a plank boardwalk. A word of caution: Wet planks can be extremely slippery.

Those hiking this trail in spring before maintenance crews have had a chance to do some housekeeping will probably encounter fallen trees over the trail, the casualties of fall and winter storms. Just be prepared for the fact that this may cut your hike short. It's always a good idea to research trail conditions before you set out to avoid any disappointment, especially in spring and fall. In winter the Asahel Curtis Nature Trail is impassable due to heavy snow-pack and downed trees.

In the right season, the sampling of so much natural diversity in such a short space and time makes this educational hiking experience one that's hard to match for both children and adults.

Miles and Directions

0.0 Start at the trailhead, located in the parking lot. Toilets are located at the trailhead.

0.4 The loop begins here; follow the trail either to the left or the right.

0.9 The loop ends; follow the signed trail back to the trailhead.

1.3 Arrive back at the trailhead.

Clubs and Trail Groups

Several environmental, conservation, and hiking resource groups are available in the Seattle area, ranging from clubs where members and participants can enjoy group outings to organizations that are happy to provide information about local trails.

The Mountaineers
The organization offers trips, classes, and events related to the Seattle-area outdoors.

7700 Sand Point Way NE
Seattle, WA 98115
(206) 521-6000
www.mountaineers.org

Issaquah Alps Trails Club
This conservation organization offers free guided hikes.

P.O. Box 351
Issaquah, WA 98027
www.issaquahalps.org

Sierra Club Cascade Chapter
Sierra Club's local chapter offers organized outings and more.

180 Nickerson Street, Suite 202
Seattle, WA 98109
(206) 378-0114
www.mountaineers.org

Washington Trails Association
The group provides information about the state's trails.

2019 Third Avenue, Suite 100
Seattle, WA 98121
(206) 625-1367
www.wta.org